Just A Simple Innkeeper
The Journey of an Irish Hotelier

Maurice Holland

Copyright © 2019 (Maurice Holland)
All rights reserved worldwide.

No part of this book can be stored, changed, sold, copied or transmitted in any form or by whatever means other than what is outlined in this book without the prior permission in writing of the person holding the copyright, except for the use of brief quotations and certain other non-commercial uses permitted by copyright law.

Publisher: Inspiring Publishers,
P.O. Box 159, Calwell, ACT Australia 2905
Email: publishaspg@gmail.com
http://www.inspiringpublishers.com

A catalogue record for this book is available from the National Library of Australia

National Library of Australia The Prepublication Data Service

Author: Maurice Holland
Title: Just A Simple Innkeeper
Genre: Non-fiction
ISBN: 978-1-925908-84-8

This journey started in the summer of 1964, in Monaghan, Ireland. Monaghan was what is referred to as a market town. It was surrounded by agricultural land, where farming was the main stay of the local economy. Farmers came to town to sell their produce and livestock, replenish their stock of groceries, hardware, and clothing, and to partake of copious amounts of beer in the local pubs.

There were designated market days in the town, when the sidewalks would be lined with wagons offering sheep, pigs, and all sorts of fowl for sale. Horses and cattle were also featured, with designated spots where they stood for inspection. Obviously, this display of livestock produced mountains of horse, cow, and pig shit, and rivers of urine, which accumulated on the sidewalks throughout the day. It was not a pleasant sight, and an enormous cleaning job for the council workers the day after the sales. I recall walking to school and trying to avoid mountains of horse and cow manure on the pavements.

But it was all in the spirit of good wholesome commerce, and was, at that time, vital to the survival of the town. Market days are a thing of the past now and, like the rest of the country, the town has flourished since Ireland's entry into the European Union.

Notwithstanding the raw vitality of market days, the town was quite pretty in its own way. It featured a number of very pleasant squares, a canal, a very impressive cathedral, and was surrounded by lakes and streams. As children, we spent summers roaming freely through hills and dales. Summers were endless. We swam in the lakes and fished in the rivers. We played football, robbed orchards and hunted for rabbits, and despite a very obvious scarcity of money, we had an idyllic childhood. I must say that I loved that town, and its wonderful down to earth, humorous, and very generous people.

My great grandfather had been a big shot in the town. He owned a pub, grocery store, land, and 16 houses. However, his son, my grandfather, managed to lose the lot somehow. And no explanation for the loss could be determined despite enquiries made by my brother and sister. Those who knew the details have all passed on, so we will never know, I suppose. Strange!

We were never really conscious of money, or the lack of it. Almost every family in town struggled somewhat to make ends meet. Ireland was a very young nation those days, with limited industrialisation. Jobs were hard to come by, and those lucky enough to have one were paid minimal wages. However, families survived from day to day, and somehow managed to feed and clothe tribes of children.

This experience made children quite independent and determined to somehow succeed. I recall that my school buddy, Joe, and I were quite entrepreneurial. We collected and sold scrap metal, hunted for return bottles in the town dump, sold holly at Christmas, worked at the hay in summer, and generally managed to be quite self-sufficient where pocket money was concerned.

In those days, there existed a very interesting source of income for a number of the townsfolk. This derived from the fact that Monaghan was, and is, located right on the border between the Republic of Ireland and the UK controlled Northern Ireland. The price of goods between the two tended to vary considerably. This gave rise to a very significant smuggling trade back and forth across the border. Food, alcohol, tobacco, fuel, and livestock were all fair game. Butter, in particular, was continually smuggled from the north into the south, as the price was subsidised in Northern Ireland by the British government, making it considerably cheaper than the same product in the south.

The smugglers were quite wonderful characters, and were prepared to drive trucks full of goods on byroads back and forth. They were often chased by police and customs officers and had to, from time to time, abandon a truck and head for the fields, with the constabulary in full pursuit. The families involved in this trade were somewhat admired by the townsfolk for their ingenuity and bravery.

Starting Out.

Having just completed my final year of secondary school in 1964, I was one of many awaiting the results of final examinations. The results would, to a great extent, determine my job prospects. So some degree of anxiety pervaded my thoughts.

I had struggled somewhat at school due to an administrative decision on the part of the school authorities. My first year class in secondary school was too large for the classroom, so the administrators, in their questionable wisdom, promoted three students to the second year class. I was one of them.

This resulted in quite significant disadvantage to the three students involved. Confronting subjects such as science, algebra, and the rest of the secondary school agenda, without having learned the fundamentals was indeed challenging. There was no tutoring to help us. We were left to our own designs and somehow expected to handle the situation. The stress level was significant each and every day at school, as we simply could not grasp the lessons. In fact, it was so challenging that my two colleagues quit school after only one year. I managed to survive, but not without some difficulty simply trying to keep up.

Under pressure to absorb as much as quickly as possible, I tended to skim through school books trying to identify the critical elements. I also lived in a certain fear of the teachers, who on the whole were not particularly patient with my dilemma.

I subsequently have always had a problem communicating upwards, which of course may have been due to a natural shyness, but I fear it had more to do with my schooling experience, and fear of the teachers. To this day, I feel that I suffered personal consequences related to my personality, my education, and my future prospects.

All that said, there are many people in the world who have had significantly worse experiences in their youth than mine, so I am always conscious of life's blessings, and there have been many, to which I will relate as this parable unfolds.

The Leaving Certificate examination was a seven subject exam with a Pass or Honours mark, depending on performance. I had ambitiously chosen to seek honours in six subjects and pass in one, mathematics. An Honours result tended to translate well in the jobs market.

I recall a bright Sunday morning after church being advised by friends that the results had been announced the previous evening. Trepidation invaded my being, and I had to wait until the following day to get the results. A sleepless night, but to my great surprise and relief I passed with Honours!

Job offers started to evolve, as hoped. One attractive option was a position as an officer with the local council. A secure appointment with promotion prospects, and a good pension scheme. My family encouraged me to accept, which seemed my best option.

However, I was vaguely aware of a university scholarship scheme offered to graduating students by the county council. Tertiary education those days was not free in Ireland, and my family could simply not afford the expense. There were four scholarships to university, and four to what were known as Institutes of Technology. The top eight in the county were offered these scholarships. I was ninth, so missed out, I thought. However, the eighth placed student decided to pursue a teaching career, and I was therefore offered the eighth scholarship.

This unexpected development caused both joy and significant concern for my parents. My father was a postal worker on small wages, and while the scholarship paid my college fees, there was the considerable burden of funding my board and lodgings. Ours was a traditional large Irish Catholic family of seven children, with three still at school. We never wanted for food and clothing, but there was never any money for extras. Providing financial support through college for one of the children was not in the planning. Regardless, I was encouraged to explore the options at the various colleges.

The scholarship was provided to one of the Institutes of Technology in Dublin. Courses offered included engineering, architecture, planning, and the like. I had little interest in any of these and sought something more tactile, more people orientated.

One college featured an interesting option, Hotel Management. I had no background in hotels, nor was I particularly interested in the culinary arts, and had no exposure whatsoever to the finer things in life. I had organised tennis dances at the local hotel, and was mindful of the role played by the manager. The job seemed to revolve around the reception desk, and the restaurant and bar. Some administration was surely a requirement, but I was not familiar with this, as my interaction with the manager was limited to booking my dances, agreeing on a price, and a start and finish time. However, the manager seemed to be a contented and pleasant person, outgoing, and people orientated. And how hard could it be?

Introduction

I contacted the college and was invited for an interview at St Mary's College of Catering and Domestic Science.

In addition to Hotel Management, there were courses in Dietetics, Institutional Management, Cookery Apprenticeships, and Event Management. The college was known by its street address, Cathal Brugha Street, the street being named in memory of a hero of the Irish struggle for independence.

The Domestic Science referred to a one year course where young ladies from the higher echelons of Dublin society learned the finer points of conducting a household. It was akin to a finishing school, preparing the ladies for society, and married life. This feature was an added bonus, as these ladies tended to be happy go lucky socialites who greatly enhanced the social life of the college.

Attending the interview involved what was then the significant and costly journey to Dublin, which is located approximately 100 kilometres from Monaghan. In order to avoid the expense of travel, my father arranged a lift for me with the local greengrocer, Frank Brady, who journeyed to the Dublin markets regularly to pick up produce. I was accompanied on the journey by a great school friend, Matt Gallagher, who had also secured a scholarship and was attending an interview.

Frank, the greengrocer, was a great philosopher, and a very slow driver. We departed Monaghan at 6am and arrived in Dublin at noon, having listened to Franks wisdom and assisted him with deliveries to various customers on the way. Frank considered himself a careful driver with the motto 'better 30 minutes late than 30 years too soon'. I think we averaged 20 kilometres per hour.

Fortunately, my interview was in the afternoon. It was conducted by the college principal, Miss Boucher Hayes. An elegant lady possessed of great insight, who ruled the college with a certain discipline designed to uphold its reputation.

She enquired as to my interest in hotel management and went to great lengths to point out the limited prospects involved in the profession, together with the drudgery of long hours for little wages. She pointed out that I had the option to study more established career paths such as engineering or architecture, and that the rewards of those pursuits might be greater in the long run. Was I sure about my choice, she asked. To this day I do not know why I was so determined to pursue a career in hotels, but I indicated that my mind was made up, and that an innkeeper I would be. Miss Hayes bowed to my naivety and welcomed me to her flock.

Dublin

College commenced in September. My school friend Matt and I were again transported to Dublin by the greengrocer. We arrived with no lodgings and a total lack of familiarity with the nation's capital. Obviously, the first priority was therefore to find a place to sleep. Cost was the major consideration in our search, and we managed to find dormitory style accommodation in a boarding house in Synge Street, famous as the birthplace of one illustrious Irishman, George Bernard Shaw. The house opposite our lodgings featured a plaque commemorating the great writer's birth.

Thinking back I greatly admire the relaxed confidence my parents had in their 17 year old son. I had journeyed to Dublin with my friend Matt with very little money, no idea as to where we would find accommodation, and with very limited knowledge of the city. I doubt if today's parents would be so relaxed, but then society was very different in those days.

There were six beds in every room, somewhat like modern day back packing. Breakfast was included and since lunch was provided at my college, I was ahead of the game. All I needed was the weekly rent and the bus fare. However, the six to a room situation became somewhat uncomfortable after a short while, and we embarked on a search for alternative accommodation.

As coincidence would have it, one of our room mates, Ken Kingston, was enrolled in the same course as myself, and he indicated that he too would be happy to join us in some alternative arrangement that met budget considerations. Ken struck me as being somewhat more mature than us. He smoked, drank, and was a man of the world. He also spoke fluent Gaelic. He was good company. Our search resulted in the three of us sharing part of a family house, with one bedroom and lounge room, located in the convenient suburb of Phibsboro. It was very basic, but convenient and cheap, and we were now three to a bedroom instead of six.

The College

St Marys College of Catering and Domestic Science was an institution staffed by outstanding administrators and lecturers. The Hotel Management faculty featured subjects in restaurant service, cookery, dietetics, wine knowledge, cost control, management principles, economics, accounting, and law.

Among the teachers were industry doyens who had led successful careers in some of Irelands and Europe's best hotels. Head Chefs, Head Waiters, published cooks, functioning lawyers, accountants, and dietitians, all made contributions to our introduction to, and education in, the hotel industry. And this was no easy task given the raw material these illustrious teachers had to work with.

Most of my class colleagues were from country Ireland. Some had tried other careers and either failed or simply sought new horizons. Most were totally uninformed, with little or no knowledge of the industry. It must have been a considerable challenge for an individual experienced in the finer points of luxury hotel service to attempt to impart such knowledge and sophistication to the sons and daughters of postmen and farmers.

Most of my classmates were like myself, brought up in rough and tumble family situations, where table manners were pretty basic, and food was only ever considered as nourishment to keep body and soul together. The world of hotels and the refined atmosphere of Cathal Brugha St was a strange place indeed.

Our first year at the college was an introduction to the fundamentals of the industry. These initial teachings related to restaurant service and cooking, together with lessons in cost control, and an introduction to dietetics. Interesting that dietary considerations were included in the course so long ago. Quite an enlightened aspect of the curriculum.

Much time was spent in the presence of the suave and sophisticated restaurant manager, Kevin O'Rourke. This gentleman had spent his entire career in luxury hotel restaurants, and was possessed of an encyclopaedic knowledge of the finer points of restaurant service. He was a patient and enthusiastic teacher, who spent endless time and effort teaching us the rudiments of service, which included setting tables, carrying plates, folding napkins, which side to serve and clear, and how to greet and treat customers.

From there we graduated to the finer points of Service a l'Anglaise, Service a la Francaise, and Service a la Russe. These methods of service had evolved from the great houses of Europe and had been, in a way, handed down to the luxury hotel world.

Nowadays service tends to be limited to English style, which involves a waiter serving food from a platter to each guest, or French style, where a number of dishes are placed on the dining table at the same time, for the guests to help themselves, sometimes referred to as family style. Of course, there are various other methods of serving food such as plate service, buffets and the like. But in the luxury world, English service tends to be the norm.

However, most free standing restaurants now use simple plate service where the food comes from the kitchen already arranged on a plate. This method was frowned upon in former days, but chefs now prefer it as they have the final say on how the food is presented on the plate. Waiters tend to mess things up serving from a platter!

O'Rourke also regaled us with fascinating stories of the luxury hotel world. Grand banquets, royal events, giant personalities, famous chefs, and simply the hedonist mystery of it all conjured up dreams of a fascinating career for all of us. I must say that I was immediately smitten by the whole affair. I actually felt, perhaps, like an innocent country boy entering into service in one of the great houses of yesteryear. Yes, I was being trained to provide sophisticated service to wealthy clients but I loved it. I was entranced by the whole experience. I have always loved the industry. The sheer humanity of it has always been intoxicating.

Within a few weeks we became competent enough to embark on the nerve racking task of serving the teacher customers in the dining room. This was indeed an intimidating experience, as we were being observed by the teachers, and the illustrious O'Rourke, at the same time. Frequent accidents occurred, of course, with food or beverage ending up in teachers laps. Young lads from the country trying to master silver service using a spoon and fork to serve meat and vegetable creations from a silver salver to a dining plate, was fraught with danger. The teachers, however, were mostly understanding, although going back to college with food stains was not exactly their expectation. But the teachers did enjoy a free lunch of generally excellent food, so I dare say it was worth the risk.

Next we embarked on our mission in the kitchens. Learning to cook was a fascinating experience. This was cooking of a type that none of us had ever experienced. The Repertoire De La Cuisine, written by a student of the great chef, Escoffier, and essentially recording Escoffier's menus and methods, was to become our reference. Escoffier was known as the King of Chefs and the Chef of Kings. He simplified French food adding fresh ingredients and modernising the ornate style. Escoffier was the director of cooking at the Savoy in London when it opened.

However, before we were permitted to embark on anything close to a sophisticated creation, we were schooled in the basics. This included lessons on how to wear a chefs uniform, how to peel potatoes, how to chop parsley, and so on. Not all of my classmates were natural cooks, which became quite evident in the early stages.

On the other hand, one or two had the natural gift, and excelled in the kitchens throughout the course. Indeed, one in particular, Jim Morris, became a noted restauranteur in Stratford, Canada, owning and operating a wonderful and renowned restaurant and cooking school, known as Rundles.

The majority of us made a worthwhile effort, and mastered much of what was being presented. Items produced in the kitchens were either served to the teachers in the dining room or provided to the students in the cafeteria. Often we would be served the food we had cooked prior to lunch, so if it was not up to standard, we had no one to blame but ourselves.

On one occasion we had been introduced to the art of cooking game. The game consisted of pheasant, snipe, rabbit, and various other extraordinary items. All of it had been 'hung' which really meant it had been allowed to ferment to a point where a pungent smell was obvious, and a few maggots too. This process is greatly appreciated by connoisseurs of game meat, but was certainly not to our liking. Unfortunately, when we got to the cafeteria for lunch, our game dishes were what we were served. I never did develop the taste.

Domestic Life

Life in our lodgings was pretty basic. We were all dependent upon a weekly postal delivery of funds from home. This normally arrived on a Friday. Apart from rent money, there was just enough to pay for food. And the walk to college was only about five kilometres, so there was no need to spend money on the bus. We got by, as long as the money arrived on the Friday.

On one occasion it was delayed and I recall that my total funds amounted to two shillings and sixpence, or the old half crown, 50 cents in today's money. Not much to get through the weekend, but I thought I could buy a couple of eggs and a loaf of bread, and that would solve any hunger issues.

My two flatmates were in a similar bind. Obviously, something had gone wrong with the Irish postal service. They too were skint of funds. However, they had a greater dilemma than me. They both smoked and faced the prospect of a whole weekend without a nicotine charge. They were aware that I had some meagre funds which I intended spending on food, so they set about convincing me to buy cigarettes instead.

I resisted for a while, but then, after much beseeching from my deprived mates, I gave in and bought a packet of Carrols Number One, instead of the food. This brought great cheer to the two desperates, but it left all three of us without anything to eat for the weekend. A sad prospect indeed. However, where there is life there is always hope.

The next morning I decided to walk to the college to see if I could scrounge a lunch in the cafeteria, although we were not entitled to dine on the weekends. I sauntered down the streets of Dublin engaged in my usual preoccupation of looking at car number plates. I don't know why, but all my life I have been able to remember the number plates of most of my friends cars. Low and behold, I spotted a very familiar number plate. It belonged to my wonderful sister Nora's fiancé, Sean McCionna.

The happy couple were obviously in Dublin for a romantic weekend, and I am sure the last person they wanted to see was the feckless brother. Regardless, I raced after the car and managed to catch up with them at a traffic light. They feigned great delight at seeing me, but it was nothing compared to my relief in seeing them.

I was treated to lunch at the Paradiso restaurant, and when departing, my beautiful sister gave me a whole five pounds. Wow! I was set for the weekend. And my flatmates shared in the spoils when I brought home milk, bread and a few other staples to see us through and, of course, another pack of cigarettes!

Galway

For the duration of the first college summer break, we were expected to gain practical restaurant experience working in a college approved hotel. A number of major hotels had a tradition of employing college students for the summer period. The college generally represented a source of keen and enthusiastic workers, suitable to assist the hotels over the traditional summer tourist season.

Three colleagues and I chose the Great Southern Hotel in Galway, a thriving tourist destination and fine hotel on Ireland's west coast. We were employed as commis waiters, which is basically on the lowest rung of the hotel hierarchy. The term 'commis' refers to an apprentice, so we were apprentice waiters. In luxury restaurant operations the commis carries the food from the kitchen to the dining room, sets and clears tables, and generally handles all the menial jobs the experienced waiters consider beneath them.

I was attached to a wily character called John Lally, who had worked in the main dining room of the hotel for many years. Lally was a hard task master and had little time or patience for college students. He was gruff, and barked instructions endlessly. But I was a fast learner and responded to Lally's instructions efficiently. I carried large trays of food from the kitchen, quickly cleared tables, and generally anticipated Lally's orders.

One order I recall was my duty to gather and save tea spoons. I don't know why, but for generations tea spoons were a scarce commodity in most busy hotel dining rooms. Waiters tended to gather and store them in their pockets, and most times they were unwashed. Perhaps this is why there was a shortage! In any case, I became quite adept at finding spoons, much to Lally's delight.

My waiting skills were improving, and within a short period, I could carry three plates in one hand and a fourth in the other. However, I had difficulty mastering the technique of carrying three plates with a glass of liquid on each, all in one hand. I could carry two, and a third in the other hand but this was not very efficient, as I would have to return to the kitchen for the fourth item, if there were four people dining.

One of my fellow workers, a Swiss gentleman named Jimmy Casada, knew of my difficulty in this regard and kept teasing me as I ran back and forth. Jimmy of course was a master of the art and could carry any array of dishes with a flourish.

One day I was required to serve four glasses of tomato juice on plates with doyleys, to a party of American tourists. Jimmy was close by and challenged me to carry all four at once. I could not resist, so I set off with three plates balanced precariously in one hand, and one in the other. I got through the double doors to the restaurant which was no mean feat, and approached the table. One of the party was a rather large and buxom lady who was sitting somewhat side on to the table. I chose her to serve the first juice and just as I was laying it on the table the glass wobbled. I reacted instinctively by trying to right the wobbly glass which resulted in all four glasses of tomato juice tumbling onto this lady's bosom.

I was mortified, and so shocked that I almost made the situation worse by my inclination to wipe down the front of her dress. Fortunately, I didn't, and in any case the lady had recoiled in horror as she anticipated my thought process. Of course, the head waiter and all sorts of managers were on the scene immediately, offering profuse apologies. I was feeling like the biggest dope, and hoping the floor would open up and swallow me. And out of the corner of my eye I could see Jimmy giggling to himself.

Commis waiters were given the task of handling the room service breakfast shift, a 6am start with breakfast served from 7am. As young men enjoying the summer in a happening place like Galway, we were often out late at night. So early rising was often a challenge. However, if we slept in, we would be awakened by the thunderous voice of the head waiter, Pat Lawless, banging the door and screaming 'any chance lads, any fucking chance'. What a wake up!

Room Service breakfast was fun, and it was interesting to find hotel guests in various states of undress, and not remotely bothered. The waiters tended to be more embarrassed than the customers.

The room service trays had to be collected after breakfast, and this could be quite lucrative as many of the guests left cash tips on the them. There was one waiter who got further enjoyment from this exercise, as he would open the window of the room and pelt boiled egg leftovers at innocent strollers in Eyre Square. Complaints to the hotel management were met with disbelief, and a suggestion that it must have been birds dropping the missiles. It could not have come from the Great Southern. Certainly not!

After three months working at the Great Southern we had become quite competent in the skills of restaurant and hotel banquet service. It was now time to return to college. We left the hotel on good terms, and were invited back to work during the weekend of the Galway Oyster Festival, which we gladly accepted.

Second Year

The second year of college was essentially more of the same but at a higher level. We could now operate efficiently in the restaurant and had absorbed the basics of the culinary world. Our three months in real hotel situations had bestowed a certain confidence in all of us, although some bad habits picked up through the summer had to be corrected.

We spent more time in the college kitchens developing our cooking skills. We also began to focus on more weighty subjects such as management principles, cost control, law, economics, accountancy and dietary considerations.

I had moved to more salubrious accommodation with two colleagues who were to become great friends in later life, Billy Munnelly, who became a renowned wine expert, and Jim Morris of the restaurant fame, and my school friend, Matt. Now we were only two to a room so things were looking up. In addition, our skills as experienced waiters resulted in many of us gaining casual evening work at the illustrious Shelbourne Hotel in Dublin, where we served at the various banquets. I had saved a little money from my summer work, and together with the income from the Shelbourne, it meant that I no longer required any funding from my parents. I can only imagine what an enormous relief this must have been for them.

Part Time Work.

Work at The Shelbourne entailed the service of food and beverage at the many dinners held at this popular and refined hotel. Most society annual balls took place there and to my knowledge, still do. Customers were normally wearing evening dress and we, the waiters were in similar garb. They were grand affairs. Our role included taking drink orders, collecting payment for said drinks, and serving the meals. Each waiter was required to pay the bar for drink orders and then collect from the customers. That way it was up to the waiter to ensure that he collected the money, otherwise he would be out of pocket. So, it is easy to understand why the waiters were eager to ensure that drink bills were paid.

On one chaotic occasion I was paired to work with Frank Flaherty, a fond college friend. Frank was and is a larger than life character, a trait which has caused him some angst from time to time. On this occasion we were allotted two large tables with 20 customers, on the balcony overlooking the dance floor. In between these two tables was what is referred to as a 'gueridon' or serving table. This table is for the use of the waiters to distribute the food from very large platters onto plates, which are then delivered to the customers. With

40 customers to serve in this fashion we had our work cut out, particularly as we also had to serve drinks.

Frank decided to take control of the situation and advised me that he would handle the drinks, while I prepared for the food service. I busied myself with arranging the plates and serving utensils, and serving the first course of food, a simple hors d'oeuvre type starter which I could handle on my own. Frank embarked on providing alcohol to the thirsty customers.

All seemed under control until it was time to serve the main course. This required full attention from both of us. We went to the kitchen to collect the large and very hot platters of meat, sauce, and vegetables, and made our way back to the serving table. To our astonishment, there were six customers sitting at the service table with cutlery and napkins, awaiting dinner. There had been an oversight in the booking system, and these unfortunate people did not have a table allocated to them. The head waiter in his wisdom commandeered our serving table, placed six chairs around it and set it with cutlery. It was a very cosy fit indeed for six people. In addition, it made getting to the two large tables very difficult due to the cramped space.

So here we were loaded down with large platters and nowhere to place them. The head waiter could sense the dilemma, so he instructed us to place the platters on the stairway which led up to the next level balcony and serve from there. Just imagine the situation. The steps were covered in platters of food and plates. Frank and I, along with the head waiter and his assistant, attempting to transfer the food onto the plates in some presentable form, while trying not to spill the gravy. We failed of course, resulting in sticky gravy all over the stairway.

In the middle of this chaos, the customers started calling for more drinks which the bold Frank promptly took care of, paying the bar out of his own pocket with a mind to collecting from the customers later. Frank felt that if he could get a few drinks into them then they would be more relaxed, and not too concerned about the mayhem they were witnessing in the service of their meal. So, bottles of wine, beer and various cocktails were served and the customers did indeed seem to relax.

The headwaiter had assigned other staff to assist me in completing the food service, so some order was being restored. However, the food was somewhat spoiled to say the least, and the customers took to the dance floor, or went to tell friends at other tables of their woeful experience.

This is when Frank started to become nervous about his outstanding drink bills. Some customers seemed to be gone for a very long time and we wondered if they had joined other tables, or indeed left the premises. Frank asked me to survey the dance floor with him to check if I recognised any of our customers. I did not, but Frank was certain that he recognised a certain customer. Frank rushed to the dance floor and immediately accosted this unfortunate gentleman, who was merrily dancing the night away with his partner. Frank accused him of not paying his drink bill, to which the customer replied that he was not even sitting in that part of the ballroom, but was with friends in another section.

The head waiter was called to restrain the excited Frank, and to appease the customer, who was offered champagne and other inducements in the hope that he would forgive this harsh intrusion in his otherwise enjoyable evening. Frank never did find all the people who owed him money, unfortunately, and spent many evenings working in order to recoup his losses. Despite such challenges, Frank carved out a very successful career in the industry, culminating with a long period as General Manager of the the very elegant Majestic Hotel in Harrogate, England.

Becoming Chefs

For the duration of the second summer break we were again required to find employment in a college approved hotel. However, this time it was as apprentice chefs, not waiters. A dear friend Matt Sherlock and I managed to secure positions in the kitchen of The Great Danes Hotel, in a beautiful part of Kent, the garden of England.

At that time the hotel was owned by the Rank Organisation, and was of a very high standard. Situated in its own grounds, surrounded by manicured lawns, the hotel had a good reputation, and attracted business from tourists, weddings and an assortment of conferences and meetings. It tended to be especially busy during the summer season.

Our journey to Kent was quite eventful. Those were the days of expensive air travel when some entrepreneurial individual dreamed up the concept of student flights. These were essentially cheap charters organised through somewhat dodgy airlines, and offering a basic flight in a very basic aircraft.

In our case we were booked to travel from Dublin to Heathrow departing at 2pm, which would allow us ample time to catch the train from Victoria station to Maidstone, where hotel transport would be provided. When we arrived at Dublin airport we were advised that due to the unexpected high number of passengers booked on the flight there would be a delay, as the plane was overloaded, and some excess fuel had to be removed. How they did not know the exact number of passengers prior to fuelling is beyond me.

In any case, a further complication arose when it was discovered that only a specialised fuel truck could be used to take fuel from a plane, and such a truck was not readily available at the airport. This issue had something to do with contamination. Who knows?

The more I think of those student flight scenarios the more I wonder if the organisation was being run by students, and that perhaps even the pilot was a student. It was all very amateurish and, possibly, dangerous.

So, we waited and waited. There was absolutely no ongoing advice to the exasperated passengers. Just a sign saying 'delayed'. Eventually, we were advised that the flight would be taking off at 10pm. This now presented us with the dilemma of missing the last train to Maidstone, and being stranded in London with very little funds at our disposal. Certainly not sufficient to pay for overnight accommodation.

We arrived at Heathrow with some relief and decided to make our way to Victoria station hoping there was a later train. Of course there wasn't. We were stranded. It was after midnight and here we were with our suitcases and nowhere to sleep. The only option seemed to be a station bench so we gave it a go. After an hour or so on the hard benches we gave up.

Just then we were approached by a friendly cleaner who recognised our dilemma and suggested that we could sleep in one of the trains, as long as we were out of there by 6am, as the train was departing for Edinburgh at 7am and passengers would be arriving early. We were very grateful to this kind person and settled ourselves in a first class carriage. It was pretty comfortable and we dozed off very quickly, totally exhausted.

I was awakened next morning by someone shaking me, and when I opened my eyes I was staring up at a London bobby. In his uniform and helmet he seemed huge, and he was also quite unsmiling. 'Out' he snarled, 'or you'll be up before the magistrate'. I was terrified. Grabbing my suitcase I jumped from the train, as did Matt.

To our surprise, the platform was crowded with other 'dossers' as we called them. Dosser was the term for someone sleeping rough on someone else's premises. Still is, I think. Seemingly, it was a regular early morning duty for the London police to clear the trains of these freeloaders. And there we were thinking that we were the only ones.

We were very relieved to catch the train to Maidstone, where we were collected by the hotel, and ensconced in homely accommodation in Rose Cottage, the home of a very lovely English lady who would be our landlady for the next three months.

The Hotel Kitchen

We started work immediately at the Great Danes. We knew how to dress in the chefs uniform, but we discovered, however, that we did not know much about cooking in a very busy hotel. What we had learned at college was quality orientated, but not really practical in terms of operating in a fast and furious kitchen. So, we had to learn fast.

I recall one very embarrassing occasion when I was asked to cook some chips, which should not have been a major challenge. However, the thought struck me that I had never before cooked chips so I became somewhat anxious. Feeling really stupid, I asked the chef how to know when chips are cooked. He yelled at me, ' when they float, you idiot'. I never forgot that lesson.

Similar to our experience as commis waiters in the restaurant, we eventually got the hang of the kitchen and started to make a meaningful contribution. The head chef developed some trust in us and we were now running our own kitchen section or, indeed, handling the cooking at the hotel grillroom. Grill operations are simpler than fine dining of course, so we developed confidence quite quickly. However, we were also involved in the main kitchen where the fine dining food was produced. The hotel had a very good restaurant with an outstanding reputation.

Restaurant kitchens vary greatly in how they are operated, but in those days the main kitchen was divided into sections with a chef in charge of each section. Usually the sections consisted of the cold section and larder, meat section, vegetable section, and desserts. There are variations to these arrangements but essentially each section specialised and focused on a certain part of the menu.

I really enjoyed the buzz in the kitchen on busy evenings with the head chef barking orders and each section chef acknowledging. Orders piling up, waiters clamouring for dishes, chefs abusing them, and everybody simply striving to satisfy the customer. I loved it.

As apprentice chefs, it fell to us to operate the breakfast shift. This could be a busy operation when the hotel rooms were fully booked, as they often were. And the breakfast menu was very comprehensive offering a wide range of breakfast fare including English favourites like smoked haddock with poached eggs on top. Kippers, lambs fry, porridge, eggs, bacon and sausages were in high demand. But it was essentially simple to handle as long as one was organised in advance. This organisation involved having trays of raw materials ready in the fridge and simply cooking them under the grill, on an as needed basis.

On one rather challenging occasion I was in the midst of a very busy breakfast when the head waiter announced that a tourist coach had arrived unexpectedly, and required bacon and eggs for a party of 50. This was in addition to the 140 or so hotel guests! A certain panic gripped me but I managed to tray up additional food items, and embarked on preparing the rather large order for bacon and eggs.

Just then a waiter ordered a portion of porridge which surprisingly was the first order for porridge that morning.

I realised then that I had forgotten to make the porridge. Thinking too quickly, I grabbed a bag of oats, flung them into a pot and filled the pot with boiling water from the kitchen still. Stirred feverishly and produced a creamy porridge.

Having served the portion I left the spoon in the pot and put it to one side in anticipation of other orders. Sometime later a second order was made and I grabbed the pot to dish it up. The spoon was stuck like concrete so I had to use more boiling water to loosen it and reconstitute the porridge. I served it and got on with the bacon and eggs project.

Later on a third order for porridge was made and the same thing happened. The porridge in the pot had again solidified and the spoon was stuck again. More boiling water and hey presto I had creamy porridge. However, this episode made me think about the earlier customers who had eaten my porridge concentrate. I have no doubt that they must have suffered severe constipation as a result of my creations.

I enjoyed the kitchen experience and, apart from the porridge debacle, I was quite competent. In fact, the head chef asked me to consider a career as a chef rather than going back to college. I gave this due consideration but thankfully decided to pursue my management career.

Final Year

Back at college we were now the seniors. The curriculum by this stage was entirely classroom based with no further practical sessions as cooks and waiters. However, we were honoured with roles as head waiters, head chefs, sommeliers, and restaurant managers at the various functions held at the college.

Student politics entered my life at this stage and, to the surprise of my classmates, I decided to run for student president. This entailed a period of electioneering, including distribution of pamphlets, posters, and even my flatmate Jim's bedsheet plastered with Vote for Holland inscriptions on the day of the vote. I smiled and chatted to the girls, entered debates, and generally made an effort to lift my profile. And it worked.

I was elected college president. This role entailed chairing of the student council, representing the college at student union events, and generally overseeing the various college activities like debating, sports and entertainment. I enjoyed the role immensely and must say that it cast me into a situation which greatly improved my confidence.

The final year rolled by very quickly and before we knew it we were approaching the end. Final exams took place in May of 1967 and after that we were released into the real world. I was honoured at graduation by being presented with the gold watch for outstanding progress in my final year. I am sure my stint as student president influenced the adjudicators.

St Marys College of Catering was a fulfilling experience. I left there bestowed with an appreciation of the finer things in life, and an enthusiasm for the wonderful world of hotels. I also left having spent three years with fellows who would become lifelong friends. At the time of writing, 2019, my college mates and I have just recently completed our latest reunion in Ireland, some 50 years after graduation. And our reunions have been regular and enjoyable occurrences throughout the years, with yet another planned for 2020. Not many college fraternities can boast such comradeship, I suspect.

Chollerford

Having left the care free student life, we were now faced with finding real employment in the industry. We had been educated in the theoretical principles of management but our practical experience related to cooking and waiting. Most college graduates seek further training with the larger hotel companies, who run graduate programmes in order to foster a future source of managers. Other companies simply offer graduates junior positions in management and leave them to their own design in terms of developing management skills, often through association with senior managers. This latter option is not the best, and can result in the graduate being used as cheap labour, without much reward in terms of advancement.

A number of my colleagues and myself applied to the Trust House Forte group for admission to their then highly respected corporate trainee programme. We had interviews in London and were advised that results would be announced in September. Three of my friends, Frank Flaherty, Billy Munnelly and Jim Morris went off to England in search of temporary work, until news of a more permanent position materialised. I had arranged to join my friends at a later stage, as I was somewhat enthralled by a young lady who had invited me to join her family on vacation.

So, I arrived in London a couple of weeks later and made contact with a friend with whom my colleagues had left word of their whereabouts. Our London friend advised me that he had received a postcard from my mates which seemed to say they had found work in Chelmsford, and that I should join them there.

Unfortunately, when I got to our friends apartment and actually read the postcard the address was not Chelmsford in Essex but Chollerford in Northumberland. Chelmsford is located about one hour from London, while Chollerford is some 400 hundred kilometres north. I was again presented with the scarcity of funds scenario. The train ticket to Newcastle, close to Chollerford, would be expensive and I was down to my last few quid.

In any case, I managed to contact my mates in Chollerford and advised them that I would arrive in Newcastle the following day. I just managed to afford the train fare, and when I arrived in Newcastle I had one shilling and sixpence left, about 20 cents in today's money, which was all I had in the world! Fortunately, Frank was at the station to meet me and drive me to The George Hotel in Chollerford, which would be my home and workplace for the next three months.

The George in Chollerford

The George Hotel Chollerford is located in a very idyllic setting on a tributary to the Tyne river, with beautiful gardens, and surrounded by historic icons such as Hadrians Wall, built by the Romans. Overall a beautiful setting and frequented by visitors from Newcastle, in particular.

Fawlty Towers was a very amusing series made by John Cleese. Perhaps Cleese had experienced the George in Chollerford, and based his scenarios on his experiences there. I am advised that the hotel is now a properly managed establishment, where customers are valued and satisfied, but those days the hotel was simply chaotic. My friends and I were employed as dining room waiters.

In the summer of 1967 the hotel management was dysfunctional and customers took pot luck in terms of receiving food and service. Despite this, the hotel was always busy, especially on weekends. Perhaps customers came there once and never came back, and since this was the era before social media, there was very little advice, good or bad, available on hotel and restaurant standards in general.

The dining room was very well appointed with views out to the river, where there was boating and trout fishing. Really everything was in favour of providing customer satisfaction, but the operation simply could not perform. The Head Chef, John, was a 21 year old head case who had a very rudimentary idea of cooking. He was assisted by a Jamaican cook by the name of Leo, who also possessed a rudimentary knowledge of the job. And then there were a number of apprentices who were in training. One can imagine the value of the training these unfortunates were getting from the two 'chefs'. The food was appalling.

Almost every Saturday evening just when the restaurant was full with expectant diners, John the Chef would throw down his apron, scream some curses and advise all within earshot that he was quitting right there and then if he did not get an immediate raise in his wages. He would storm off to the manager's office and demand his money. The manager was a rather weak and incompetent individual who lived in fear of the staff in general, and John in particular. He would attempt to calm John and usually ended up paying him some cash on the spot in order to get him back into the kitchen. John would then return flashing the cash for all to see. Meanwhile the customers had been kept waiting interminably. This was a regular occurrence, and one wonders why the manager did not simply terminate John and replace him with a competent chef. Ineptitude might explain it.

Leo on the other hand worked away at his own pace. Regardless of how busy the restaurant became, Leo would not or could not move any faster than dead slow. He was also incapable of producing more than one item of food at a time. So, if a waiter had a table of four and placed an order for same, Leo would cook each item separately and demand that the waiter serve it to the customer, which resulted in the party of four receiving their meals at different stages throughout the evening. Not exactly a convivial dining experience.

Breakfast was a non - event as far as the kitchen staff were concerned. We realised very quickly that on most mornings there would be no cooks on duty to cook the breakfast. Fortunately, we were able to turn to our cooking skills to attempt to fill the gap. Frank tended to take on the role of breakfast cook. However, the very elaborate breakfast menu was not quite realistic, given the circumstances, so Frank decided that bacon egg and sausage was the special for the day, every day, with no other cooked items available. Take it or leave it. This somewhat disappointed hotel guests who were anticipating Eggs Benedict, Smoked Haddock, and the many other English breakfast delights mentioned on the menu but, alas, not available.

Given its splendid setting on the banks of the river, the hotel was a favourite Sunday destination for afternoon tea, for which the hotel charged the sum of five shillings. Tea customers filled the dining room, bar, and indeed, the lobby. There was not a spare seat in the house on most Sundays. Jimmy, the Head Waiter, worked every Sunday, personally managing this event. This struck us as somewhat odd, as in most hotels the head waiter would not bother him or herself with the menial job of serving afternoon tea. Then we figured it out!

In a casual discussion with the hotel accountant one day, we learned that the hotel recorded approximately 100 teas sold each Sunday. We knew this was wrong and woefully short of the real number, which we estimated to be around 300. Now it made sense as to why Jimmy worked the Sundays. He was head waiter and cashier, and he also completed the report for the accountant. And almost all of the bills were settled in cash those days. So, Jimmy was pocketing the cash for almost 200 teas on each occasion. Not a bad little earner for Jimmy. And more inept management, of course.

Despite the obvious functional incompetence at The George, we did gain some worthwhile experience, even if it was experience in how not to manage a hotel. I was, however, happy when the time came to move on.

Newport

The Trust House Forte group decided not to include me in their corporate training scheme. This was disappointing. Seemingly I had flunked the interview. However, they instead offered me a role as a Junior Assistant Manager in a hotel in Newport, in South Wales. This was not what I was seeking, but I thought it would give me the opportunity to learn on the job from a more experienced Manager and or Senior Assistant Manager. Those days, Senior Assistants were individuals who were in line to be promoted to a hotel manager position.

Unfortunately, and unbeknownst to me, the Senior Assistant in Newport had already been promoted, and I was to be the replacement. This was the height of personnel management incompetence. Here was I straight from college with little or no management experience, 20 years old, and expected to fill a roll which only a very experienced individual could handle.

The hotel, The Westgate, was a very busy operation of 100 rooms, large and regular banqueting trade, and the busiest bar in town. The staff were all very experienced operators, and there was certainly nothing they could learn from me. Indeed, I was the one who needed to learn, and not the one to be attempting to supervise individuals who had many years of industry experience, and knew much more than me.

What a horrible experience this turned out to be. I was completely out of my depth and struggling to perform. The hours were 7am to 4pm or 4pm until midnight daily, with each second weekend off. However, I worked from 7am until midnight on the weekends I was on duty.

I was required to do the food ordering and issuing, clean out the storerooms, relieve on reception, assist in the bar and dining room, supervise functions and even change the beer when the barrel ran out.

In fact, one of my greatest embarrassments was in my first week on the job when the barman called me and asked me to change a barrel. I had never done this before and simply had no idea. However, I proceeded to the cellar and was confronted by an array of pipes, hoses, gas bottles and barrels. How to identify the empty one? Shake them I supposed and the lightest must be the empty. This I did and managed to identify which one needed changing. It looked quite simple so I proceeded to unscrew the connection.

Unfortunately, I had not turned off the gas, so when the connection was loosened all the beer in the lines gushed out all over me. I was wearing the old fashioned hotel manager's garb of pinstriped trousers and dark jacket, which I had recently purchased. I was soaked in beer. And to add insult to injury I had taken so long that the barman arrived at the cellar and abused me for being so incompetent. He was supposed to be working for me, but he was a 60 year old experienced bartender, who had little or no time for a pipsqueak like me. I did not blame him.

As I said, I was responsible for ordering the hotel food. The chef would make out the list and I would contact the suppliers. Unfortunately, I became so stressed in the job that

I tended to forget things. On one occasion when I was having one of my rare days off, I was awakened at 6am by the chef bawling at me on the phone, 'you forgot to order the fucking sausages'. Sorry Chef, was all I could mumble!

There were very few enjoyable moments in my job in Newport. The hotel was managed by a married couple, and the managers wife was a particularly unpleasant person. She delighted in pointing out my failings, and never once offered me a word of encouragement. In fact, in a strange way I learned from her how not to treat staff members. My philosophy has always been that you treat staff as colleagues and human beings, who will give their best if motivated and treated with respect. Perhaps my stint in Newport was worthwhile in this regard.

One of the few enjoyable occasions was the visit of Her Royal Highness, Princess Margaret, to Newport. A very fine lunch was arranged at the hotel by the local council. I was designated to serve the wine to the top table. The wines were a Vieux Chateau Certan from Pomerol and a Von Kesseisstatt Riesling from Germany. I assumed the princess would be well versed in her wines so I made a great effort at learning the names of the two wines. I duly approached the princess and offered her a choice of Vieux Chateau Certan or the Kesseisstatt to which she replied, 'I will have whichever is white'. This threw me completely off guard, and I had to pause for a second to ensure that I did, in fact, pour the white. The princess was not as well versed as I expected.

I decided that in order to maintain my sanity I would have to ingratiate myself with the staff. So I made a super effort to become their support in all areas, dining room, bar, banquets, and reception. I have a reasonable sense of humour, and this helped me to build bridges. I even became quite friendly with the Chef, and he and his wife used to take me out to the pub on a regular basis. The barman became my guardian when I impressed him by breaking up a fight in his bar between two rather large sailors. The mums who worked as casual waiters in the banquet area felt sorry for me, and took me under their wing, and we had lots of laughs at their very rude jokes. In the end, I lost the struggle, and after one year in Newport I was removed from the job. I was quite relieved.

Alveston

My next assignment was in Alveston as Junior Assistant Manager at the Ship Post House Hotel. Alveston is situated in south Gloucestershire, not far from the city of Bristol, and a short distance from the Severn bridge, which leads to Wales. It is a pretty place and quintessentially English, with the village of Thornbury in close proximity.

The Ship was originally a 15th century coaching inn which had been restored, with a number of bedroom wings added. This was a somewhat simpler operation than Newport and was of a higher standard. It featured a very good restaurant and cocktail bar, but had very little banqueting space. In short, it was somewhat easier for me to manage, particularly after my baptism by fire in Newport. However, I was again on a junior assistants wage doing a senior assistants job.

I was again faced with the challenge of supervising the work of senior line managers who had vastly more experience than myself. And, again, I was the support person for all areas, and the one to call when they needed assistance. So I rotated between reception, the bar and the restaurant with visits to the storerooms for after hours issues. I also supervised wedding functions and even acted as master of ceremonies, introducing the bride and groom and the various speakers.

My work was generally enjoyable but the days were very long, starting at breakfast time and working through until closing, with a mid afternoon break. This is an aspect of the business which resulted in many college graduates deciding on a career change, and leaving the industry. Low wages, long hours and doubtful prospects were certainly not encouraging signs.

I also played the role of relief night manager at Alveston. I freely admit to being afraid of the dark, and the memories of wandering around the Ship Post House in the middle of the night are not pleasant ones. Especially having heard the stories of the older part of the complex being haunted. The hotel cat also added to the spookiness by staring in an agitated state into the darkened rooms of the old section.

The restaurant at The Ship was staffed by a group of Spanish immigrants who all seemed to come from the same village in Spain. They were a fun group and very diligent workers, led by the Head Waiter, Tani, who was a human dynamo in terms of customer service. Tani ran a very efficient operation. No customer could be allowed to depart Tani's restaurant feeling unhappy or disappointed. This simply did not happen despite the challenge from time to time from totally unreasonable and demanding clients.

On one occasion I recall an obviously wealthy individual was having lunch with his much younger and somewhat affected lady friend. The gentleman complained about the quality of each and every dish that was served. He complained about the coffee being cold, the wine being warm and the service being inattentive. Tani was at his wits end trying desperately to satisfy this disgruntled and arrogant individual. In the end, Tani apologised profusely to the customer and offered he and his guest a glass of a very rare and expensive brandy with his compliments, assuring the customer that this brandy was indeed rare and a delight to drink. The customer shrugged dismissively and told Tani to bring it.

Unfortunately, when Tani checked his bar stock he discovered that one of his waiters had inadvertently served the last remaining portions of the sacred brandy in error, not realising how precious and expensive it was. Not to be outdone, Tani decided to mix a cocktail of brandies. In the empty rare old brandy bottle he mixed Curvosier, Hennessy, Hine and whatever remnants he could find in the bar, then poured the concoction into two brandy snifters. Together with the original bottle on a tray, he delivered this creation to the disgruntled customer. The customer swirled the brandy around in his glass, took a sniff, sipped a little and said to Tani 'my good man, that brandy has saved the occasion'.

My life was much improved at Alveston and I developed some friendships among the locals. I even played a bit of rugby for the fourths, and used to visit the pub with the team in the nearby village of Thornbury.

Colchester

However, after a year in Alveston, the guardians of my career in the human resources department of the company decided that I needed some exposure to food and beverage control. This is essentially an accounting function of controlling the ordering, delivery, sale, and the auditing of revenue for a hotel's food and beverage department.

It was suggested to me that a position as Food and Beverage Controller had become available at the Red Lion Hotel in Colchester, which I should seriously consider accepting. Between the lines I read that I did not have much of an option. Despite my efforts, it seemed that the manager at Alveston was keen to secure the services of a more experienced assistant. I also realised later that the Red Lion hotel had been impatiently searching for a food and beverage controller for some time, and my minder in head office was under pressure to fill the position. So, the motivation was certainly not in the interests of my development, but in filling a position for a frustrated manager.

I have witnessed many instances of inept and downright harmful decisions on the part of corporate human resource managers throughout my career. Not only related to my own personal situation, but affecting many up and coming, and very worthwhile individuals. Being on the wrong side of, or not fitting the bias of a corporate human resource executive, can often result in an aspiring and competent individual being overlooked, or simply ignored in terms of future development.

In my opinion, the human resource function in the modern corporate world has become all too powerful, with senior executives often abdicating their responsibility in this highly critical area to their human resources representative, with such individuals not entirely equipped to handle these matters.

In any case, I accepted the job in Colchester and packed my bags. Colchester is what may be described as a market town with a very long history. It is in fact the oldest recorded town in England, and was a major Roman settlement.

The Red Lion was essentially a large pub with bedrooms and some banquet space. My office was located in the basement, in what was the beverage store. I spent my days pouring over numbers, surrounded by shelves of all the alcoholic beverages stocked by the hotel. I did monthly stock takes in the hotels three bars, and all the food and beverage store rooms and kitchens.

At one point I spent a week doing daily stock takes on a particular bar where the hotel manager suspected some misappropriation of cash on the part of the bar staff. My ongoing monitoring did produce some significant discrepancies, and the staff member was counselled and relocated, subsequently resigning his position.

I was also involved on occasion in playing a role as evening duty manager at this hotel. This is a role which essentially assists the various departments during busy periods, and deals with customer issues, as the management representative.

London Bound

After some months of counting bottles, weighing potatoes and the like, spending time in very cold fridges and freezers, and serving pints of bitter to the locals, I decided that it was time for me to make a move and to take my chances out in the world. My thoughts turned to London, and my long held view that I was trained for the upper end of the market, and should seek a position in a luxury establishment.

Acting purely on impulse borne from a certain frustration with my progress to date, I contacted my minder and requested a transfer to London, as the company owned and operated various hotels there. No positions available, I was advised. Fine, I responded, I herewith tender my resignation.

At this particular time a new manager was appointed to the Red Lion. His name was Willi Bauer and he impressed me greatly with his enthusiasm, humour, and passion for the business. Willi was disappointed that I had resigned and asked me to reconsider as he felt that there was a future for me under his guidance. I considered this but decided to continue on my way. In the short time I spent with Willi Bauer I could see that he was a true hotelier, and a leader and motivator. Years later my perception was proven right when I read of his appointment as the General Manager of London's iconic Savoy Hotel. Perhaps I should have stuck with him!

London

I was now unemployed and made my way to London. I was offered accommodation with some college friends who had rented an apartment in Priory Road, West Hampstead. The apartment was owned by people involved in the antique furniture business who, although they lived in the same building, did not seem to realise that there were five Irishmen living in their renter, and not two as the rental agreement specified. It was quite a sizeable unit, with a very large living room furnished with a selection of interesting antique furniture, and a large bedroom.

A vibrant 60s culture energised London. Student demonstrations took place almost daily against the bomb, the Vietnam War, Apartheid, and every other ailment in society. Red Rudy and Tariq Ali were the ring leaders, and seemed to control thousands of willing supporters. The US embassy in Grosvenor Square was continually blockaded by screaming students. In addition, rock music, drugs and free love were the order of the day. Girls were liberated and energised. Everybody seemed to be dressed in clownish rags from Carnaby Street. The mini skirt covered very little, and worn with knee high boots on good legs was simply stunning!

I went searching for a job and was advised by a friend to enquire at Grosvenor House on Park Lane as he understood they were recruiting. Grosvenor House was a fine establishment those days with 500 bedrooms, and an adjoining complex of 200 private apartments. Between these two was the largest hotel lobby in the world, which had originally been an actual street. The developers had managed to have the street closed and converted into the grand lobby between the two accommodation units. It was very impressive.

I had discussions with a personnel executive who offered me a position as night receptionist. This was not quite what I had in mind but I was assured that if I took on the role for six months I would be moved onto the day shift, either on reception or in reservations. I accepted.

I found it interesting that Grosvenor House those days was owned by the same company I had been working for in Newport, Alveston and Colchester, and yet when I enquired about positions in London I was advised rather offhandedly that there was nothing available. This again smacked of a human resources executive more focused on filling gaps than on the progress of his charges.

I reported for work at 11pm each evening and handed over to the day shift at 7am. My job entailed checking in any late arrivals, reconciling the rooms revenue with the audit office, preparing the arrivals for the following day, and assisting the Night Manager in his defence of the hotel from the ladies of the night. The hotel had a policy which forbid customers from having guests in their rooms after 11pm. This policy was policed by the night staff who diligently surveyed the lobby in search of any unwanted visitors.

In addition, even though the elevators were touch button automatic, there was always an elevator operator on duty assisting hotel guests to their particular floor. This service was somewhat extravagant, but Grosvenor House was a true five star property, and guests could not be expected to have to fiddle with elevator buttons! The elevator operator also kept a lookout for any unwanted late night guests.

The Night Manager was a very sophisticated and imperious British Egyptian by the name of Mister Hopper. I never knew his first name. I think he was born Mister! He ruled the night shift with an iron fist and instilled poise, elegance and service consciousness in all the night staff. Hopper loved Grosvenor House and took no prisoners when it came to ensuring that staff members delivered impeccable service. He even lost patience with customers whom he considered unfit for his beloved hotel.

I recall one occasion when I was in the company of Hopper observing the lobby traffic, he suddenly breathed an oath and rushed off across the great divide of the lobby in pursuit of a certain hotel guest. Upon accosting this unfortunate American customer in the middle of the lobby, Hopper enquired in an imperious way as to what the guest thought he was doing. The guest was perplexed and asked for further explanation. ' Your hat, Sir, uttered Hopper. Remove your hat. This is Grosvenor House'.

Even though I was working the dreaded night shift, I immediately responded to the luxury atmosphere and the endemic commitment to customer service. Here was a hotel with room service kitchens and butlers on every floor, and beautifully appointed restaurants and cocktail bars. It had the largest hotel ballroom in Europe, where many fine events took place, and an array of rooms and suites lavishly decorated with exquisite taste. I felt like I had come home. This is what I was trained for.

Unwanted Guests.

During my tenure on nights a young assistant night manager was appointed. He was very keen, and involved me in his various pursuits observing the comings and goings throughout the night.

On one occasion the elevator operator alerted the assistant manager to the fact that a certain lady had taken the elevator, and that she was certainly not a hotel guest. The assistant manager immediately jumped into another elevator and went to the floor where the lady had alighted. He was just in time to see her entering a particular room. This occurred at approximately 2am and the assistant manager called me to accompany him on the floor, in case he required a witness in dealing with the situation.

I asked him what he intended to do and he said that he was going to phone the room and insist that the guest should leave. I asked him if he was sure of the room number, it being very late in the night, and he assured me that he was. So, entering the lion's den so to speak, the young assistant manager dialled the room number. He received a rather gruff 'Yes' in response. The assistant manager introduced himself, and advised the customer that he was aware there was a guest in his room, and would he please ask the guest to leave.

The customer became extremely aggressive, denied the charge, and banged the phone down. The assistant manager dialled the room again and insisted on the guest being asked to leave, to which the customer replied that he did not have a guest in his room, and that he would see to it that the assistant manager would lose his job for this rude and aggressive interruption to the customers night of rest. He hung up the phone.

'Now what', I asked, to which he replied 'we are going to the room'. I was rather perturbed at being included in this royal 'we', I must say. In any case, we went to the room, and the assistant manager knocked on the door, which was opened by a rather large man in a dressing gown. The assistant manager insisted that there was an unwelcome guest in the room, and that she should be asked to leave.

'Come in and search my room', said the customer. We marched in with great trepidation. We searched the room, even behind the curtains and in the bathroom, and there was no sign of life. Feeling totally defeated the assistant manager was about to withdraw when he decided to open the wardrobe. This was the final insult, I thought. Low and behold there, in the bottom of the wardrobe, was a cute little lady in a state of deshabille. She smiled and blew a kiss at the assistant manager, who said he was so relieved he felt like hugging her.

He then drew himself up, and in his best British accent said 'Please Sir, ask your guest to leave. Good night'. The customer sheepishly checked out of the hotel an hour later.

A Day Job

Grosvenor House human resources were true to their commitment and six months later I was offered a position in the reservations department. This was not reception, but I was getting close. I found reservations to be great fun. The hotel was forever busy, and the switchboard used to hold all calls for reservations until 9am. Right on the dot every line in the office would light up with calls, and it stayed that way until 5pm. Of course, it was all manual systems those days, and paper booking slips were being completed at a very fast pace. I recall that there was one individual, a Frenchman called Didier, who had the challenging job of keeping the room count. He had huge charts on which he recorded all the bookings, and from time to time would roar to the team 'June 20 sold out" or 'July 17 no suites'. Occasionally, the booking slips overwhelmed Didier, and that was when certain dates became overbooked, causing a rather challenging situation for reception. I enjoyed my time in reservations and ended my stint there as team leader. I was making progress.

Reception

I finally got my opportunity to work on reception. At first, I had the rather lowly position of junior receptionist. Those days, and probably still today, hotel guests were escorted to their room by a junior receptionist. No luggage was allowed in the lobby of Grosvenor House, and the porter accessed the room through a separate service lift. The junior receptionist carried the customers briefcase, made polite conversation and explained the workings of the room. The porter would wait outside while the junior receptionist was going through his routine. Then the porter would enter with the luggage. Both junior receptionist and porter would normally receive a handsome tip for their services.

There was a very interesting method of collecting and distributing the tips on the reception desk. Junior receptionists were allowed to keep any tips which were paid in coins. But all notes had to be deposited in the reception 'trunk', which was a central repository. These note tips were collected for the week, and then distributed on the basis of seniority. The Head Receptionist got the lions share, his two team leaders were next, and then the rest was divided up among the juniors. It was actually a fair system with all parties doing quite well out of it. My basic wage was a mere 10 pounds per week but after the tips were distributed, I cleared 25 pounds.

There was one room in Grosvenor House, however, which seldom if ever produced any tips. I remember the number, 744, which was a particularly small room, more like a cupboard, as one customer described it. The door to this room banged off the bed on opening, as the bed was right behind it. We junior receptionists tended to open the door and almost push our escorted guest into the room and disappear as quickly as possible, before the guest had time to realise what a tiny room they had. I recall a rather haughty reply from one of the managers to a guest who complained. The manager said, 'one pays for service in Grosvenor House, Sir, not space'.

From time to time the Head Receptionist would become suspicious of a new junior staff member, whom he felt was not depositing the note tips in the trunk. This was unfair to all and had to be arrested. In order to verify these suspicions, the leadership team would have the suspected one escort a customer whose tipping habits they knew intimately, and who always tipped say, a five pound note. If the junior involved did not make a deposit, then the suspicion was confirmed. Soon there would be a note sent to the human resources department advising them that the particular junior was not suited to reception, and should be relocated to another department.

The Head Receptionist was Jimmy Welch. A suave and sophisticated gentleman is how I would describe Jimmy. His was quite a pressurised job, especially in the high season when the whole of London was fully booked, and Grosvenor House was no exception. In fact, the traditional way for hotels to ensure that every room was occupied every night was to over book by approximately ten percent of each day's arrivals. This allowed for changes in itineraries, cancellations, illness, delayed flights and the myriad of reasons why customers simply do not arrive on the day they are expected.

In today's world the hotels do not have to overbook deliberately as customers are required to provide a credit card number as a guarantee of the booking. In addition, corporate companies who have a contracted rate arrangement with a hotel are prepared to pay for non arrivals.

However, at Grosvenor House the policy was that all rooms must be sold, but no guest could be turned away. This presented quite a challenge to Jimmy, the Head Receptionist, who spent endless hours reviewing the details of every reservation in search of some misinformation in terms of flight details, arrival time, or indeed an incorrect date. This way he could be reasonably confident of which reservation would not arrive on that particular day, and he could sell the room to the never ending waiting list of customers who simply arrived on spec.

This exercise not only realised additional room revenue for the hotel, but significant tips for Jimmy from the grateful ones for whom he had secured a room. But it was very stressful for Jimmy, for when he made the decision to release the room, he now faced hours until the end of the day simply hoping that the reservations he had determined would not turn up did not, in fact, turn up. There were, however, occasions when the stars were not aligned, and even the reservations with doubtful details all turned up.

On these occasions Jimmy would contact his counterpart on the reception desk of the apartment complex for help. The apartments were owned by corporate companies, and various wealthy individuals. Dame Margot Fonteyn was one celebrity owner who comes to mind, and whose apartment was used when it was known she was on an overseas tour.

Such people tended to travel regularly, and only used their apartments as their base in London. The apartments were graciously furnished, and did not contain very many personal belongings of the owners. In the case of the company owned apartments, there were absolutely no personal belongings, and the apartment was essentially rather lavish hotel accommodation for travelling executives. The apartment head receptionist was well aware of his clients comings and goings, so knew exactly which apartments were vacant and could perhaps be used to assist his colleague out of trouble. In such circumstances of course, any tips would have to be shared.

Hotel Maestros.

Jimmy Welch spent many years on reception at Grosvenor House, and became the friend of many illustrious customers who came to depend upon him when they had an unexpected need to visit London, and needed accommodation. Regardless of how busy the hotel was, Jimmy could somehow find a room for his favoured customers. And even a suite of rooms from time to time, when he was confronted with the arrival of an Arab Shiek and his entourage, without reservations.

In such circumstances the pressure was significant, but so also were the tips. Jimmy's financial reward was significant; he lived in a mews flat in London, drove a Jaguar, and owned a house in the country. On various occasions he had been offered promotion to senior management, but refused the offer citing his inability to handle the pressure! It was more a case of the significant decrease in his income which bothered Jimmy, I think.

Robert Guderon was the Head Porter in Grosvenor House. He was also the world president of what is known as the Golden Keys, which is a worldwide association of Head Porters from all of the illustrious luxury hotels. This organisation holds conventions in exotic destinations like Hawaii or Hong Kong, where they discuss the trials and tribulations of head porters, or head concierge, as they have come to be known. Very serious stuff, I am sure.

Robert looked after his customers by securing bookings in restaurants which had waiting lists, tickets to sold out

London shows, Wimbledon Tennis, and concerts at the Albert Hall. He had this amazing list of contacts all over London. Of course, he was greatly rewarded for such service, not to mention the mark up on the various tickets, which he shared with his supplier. But everyone was happy. The wealthy customer got what he wanted, Robert and his supplier made a profit, and Robert in turn was presented with a hefty tip.

A number of the hotels regular customers actually made their accommodation bookings through Robert, rather than through the reservations department. They liked his personal care and his attention to their specific needs in terms of which room they would occupy.

One of his regulars was an American oil millionaire who on one occasion asked Robert to purchase a Mercedes car for him, and to pick him up at the airport. Robert arranged to have the car bought through the hotel, and duly travelled to the airport to meet his customer. Over the next couple of weeks, Robert also drove the customer to various engagements in the city.

On departure, Robert drove the customer to the airport. He then asked what he should do with the car, to which the customer replied that Robert could keep it and use it on one condition, that on his visits to London, Robert would again be his driver and look after him as he had just done. The customer only came to London once each year and for just two weeks. So, Robert was left in possession of a Mercedes 500 Estate for his personal use. This is the stuff of the luxury hotel world!

Tips and Tipping

There was what was referred to as an Information Desk in the hotel lobby. This was akin to the modern day concierge desk, where customers enquiries were handled. The information desk issued room keys, took messages, sorted and delivered mail, and sent and received telex massages on the part of the hotel customers. With no internet, telex was the modern form of communication.

The desk was manned by mature gentlemen, adept at looking after all matter of customer enquiries with detailed knowledge of London, its attractions and environs. These gentlemen were also rewarded with tips, be it for delivering mail, arranging itineraries, or indeed sending telex messages.

The telex message source of income was quite amusing. Many of the hotels customers were international business executives, who depended greatly on the telex machine for not only sending messages, but details of contracts, and similar documents. Most of this traffic tended to be of an urgent nature, and the customer usually emphasised this urgency. The information staff member, would, without fail, apologise to the customer for the fact that there was a significant delay on outgoing messages, due to the volume being handled at that time.

The customer would fret, indicating that his message had to go immediately, while obsequiously slipping a 10 pound note across the desk. The information clerk would bow graciously and advise the customer that he would do his best. Immediately after such interactions, I would notice the information clerk sitting at the telex machine, merrily typing out the message, with no obvious volume delaying his work.

Tipping as a source of reward or income is somewhat frowned upon by various people. They consider it servile, and an affront to human dignity. Why should a human being have to rely on the generosity of their fellows in order to earn a living wage? I do not agree with this philosophy and tend to believe that tipping, in most instances, is a reward for providing extra service, personal care and attention, and going the extra mile in order to satisfy a customer.

The story of the telex message and the information clerk may cast some doubt on this argument, but that was not a typical situation. Most hotel employees are naturally service orientated, but they are greatly motivated to provide exemplary service when there is the potential for financial reward. Indeed, only competent and efficient individuals are capable of surviving in a role where they need to generate tips through their own commitment to service and customer satisfaction. Non performers simply do not earn sufficient funds on which to live, as they are not customer focused. They tend to leave the industry.

This natural selection results in an efficient and well paid work force, and consequent and ongoing customer satisfaction. In the United States and Canada even the unions recognise tipping zones in hotel awards. Staff employed in what is referred to as the front of house, or customer contact areas, receive the minimum wage, as the union respects the fact that these staff members are very well rewarded through customers tips. Back of house staff receive a higher basic wage, as they are not afforded the same opportunity. Both parties seem satisfied with this arrangement.

Priory Road

My living quarters were somewhat cramped with five of us sharing one large bedroom. Rent was based on an occupancy of two persons, not five, so it was cheap! However, as we were all employed in the hotel industry, our working hours tended to vary, and we were seldom all at home at the same time. This eased the congestion, somewhat.

There was, however, the endless threat of having to pass the landlords apartment, and hoping not to be challenged over one's legitimacy as a tenant. Somehow, I managed to avoid this, and can only assume that as long as the rent was paid, and there were no disturbances, the landlord was quite content.

Such cramped circumstances, however, can create certain social challenges in terms of entertaining the fairer sex, as was demonstrated on one rather embarrassing occasion. One of my flatmates, Andy, arrived home very late one evening in the company of a young lady. He ushered her into the rather grand living room where they enjoyed a nightcap or two, having no doubt already been drinking throughout the evening.

The four flatmates were all in bed in the adjoining room and were party to the flirtatious giggling which could be heard coming from the living room. After some time the inebriated couple made their way to the bedroom, with Andy insisting that he did not like to turn the lights on when retiring. His lady friend questioned what seemed like large pieces of furniture covered in blankets, which were strewn around the room. Andy advised her that they were antique pieces, being protected from damage. They were in fact the beds of the other four occupants, but I suppose in the dark, and under the influence of alcohol, one might be deluded into thinking they were pieces of furniture.

The happy couple then retired for an evening of ecstasy, witnessed by the not so slumbering flatmates. Silence then reigned until the following morning, when the young lady opened her eyes to four beds occupied by her lover's flatmates! She let out a wailing scream, rushed to the bathroom and hightailed it out of the flat, cursing Andy as she went. The relationship, somehow, did not seem to prosper beyond that eventful evening.

We bought a car. It was a 1956 Morris Oxford and it cost the sum total of 10 pounds, or two pounds each. I was the only member of the group with a driving license, so I naturally became the dedicated driver. The others could drive, but were not licensed. In any case, I was considered the most reliable driver to get the team home after a night at the pub.

The car, though not very sound mechanically, did provide us with some fun occasions including boating on the Cam in Cambridge, a trip to Epsom for the Derby, and beach trips to Brighton. Being a rather large car, and with no seat belt rules those days, we often managed to ferry six or seven passengers on these various trips.

However, one trip to Brighton ended in rather difficult circumstances. On the way home, we stopped at a pub for some refreshments. On attempting to stop in the car park the brakes failed. The car had fortunately rolled to a stop avoiding any damage to other vehicles. However, still being some 50 miles from London, we debated the problem over a few pints in the pub. We did not of course have any roadside insurance, so help was expensive, and out of the question.

It was decided that we would continue the journey with one of the passengers manning the hand brake, which we hoped would stop the car as needed. The exit from the pub car park was down a slope onto the main road. One member of our party was dedicated to stand on the road to firstly give the all clear while stopping any oncoming traffic, if needed. I drove down the ramp, our traffic lookout then ran along and jumped into the car, and off we went to London.

The handbrake application was only marginally successful, and it became a matter of timing traffic stoppages and traffic light changes, thereby hopefully avoiding collisions. This system worked quite successfully, but as we neared London we were confronted by the Chiswick Flyover which is rather akin to a roller coaster, with a steep climb to the top, and an even steeper descent down the other side to join the main M4 motorway.

This was quite an exciting ride, I must say. I decided that the best strategy was to release the handbrake and proceed with speed, relying on the hope that traffic tends to make room, as long as everyone continues at speed. I hoped that the rather threatening appearance of the fully loaded 56 Morris Oxford careering down the ramp must surely motivate other drivers to give way. Fortunately, this is exactly what happened and we joined the oncoming traffic without incident.

It was then a matter of getting off the M4 as we approached the city, and navigating the side streets to our regular mechanics workshop. This we managed to achieve. We left the car in the driveway, knowing the mechanic would recognise it, and headed to the pub for a celebratory drink.

Travel

I was promoted on Reception to become a shift leader, and was enjoying my time and work at Grosvenor House.

However, one evening in a pub my flatmates and I got to talking about travel, and someone suggested that we should consider travelling across Europe. This seemed to be the done thing for many young people, who managed to secure the ubiquitous Volkswagon van, and take off to Turkey and beyond. The 'beyond' aspect of such a trip seemed to be very exciting. Perhaps we could travel through Russia, and even onwards to Australia from Vladivostok.

The prospects of such a venture seemed to grow in proportion to the amount of beer we consumed. But there was a certain determination developing, and we agreed to explore the possibilities. We even went to the Russian embassy to enquire if we could abandon our van in Vladivostok. This request was considered ludicrous by a rather dour USSR representative, and we were advised that the van would have to leave the country with us. One could not abandon vans in Vladivostok, under any circumstances. We found this interaction quite hilarious, as the consular official was very perplexed by such a request.

Such a trip would require funds to purchase the van, and to support us throughout the trip. It was decided that we should try to secure additional part time employment in order to generate the funds. We did exactly this and secured jobs as waiters in a rather dubious restaurant and hotel operation in Earls Court.

The hotel was owned by an Arab gentleman by the name of Garrah. His restaurant was promoted as an after theatre supper club. It was very pretentious, and frequented by the nouveau riche gentlemen of London, accompanied by very glamourous but unsophisticated lady friends. The food was awful, and prepared by an Italian cook who was a total head case, incapable of producing decent food. The restaurant featured a very comprehensive wine list but stocked very few of the items on the list. Essentially it was a choice of red or white house wine of the lowest quality charged at exorbitant prices.

All in all the operation was a con job, but the customers were very uninformed, and seemed to care little. They were happy to have a late night feed with some booze. The owner recognised our expertise and polish in terms of service skills, and between the five of us we became the mainstay of the restaurant staffing, with two or more of us working on different evenings.

However, after some time we began to worry about the fact that we had not been paid. When we challenged Garrah about this he referred us to his accountant with profound apologies. We could not find the accountant until one evening when we ran into an individual in the back stairwell who seemed to have some role in administration. We were advised that there was in fact no accountant, but that this fellow did handle the payroll. However, he had had no advice about our employment, and no record of our service to date.

We arranged to see Garrah again and demanded our money. This suave but shady individual apologised again and tried to placate us by giving us each a cheap leather wallet. Probably something he had picked up in a bazaar in the Middle East. He then suggested that he was about to purchase three more hotels, which would take his holdings to five properties in total, and he would need five managers. And there just happened to be five of us!

Obviously, Garrah was trying to con us again. We may be Irish, but we are not stupid. We advised him that if we did not receive our wages there and then we would cease work, and he would have no staff to run his restaurant. As it was close to the weekend and the restaurant was heavily booked, he acquiesced, and paid us our money. We also warned him that we expected to be paid weekly, which he arranged.

So, we established a little central fund, and saved our wages for the proposed trip. However, the project fell apart when one of our group, Kevin, decided to get married to his lovely long time girlfriend, and another was promoted in his day job, and was reluctant to miss further career opportunities.

That left, Billy, Jim, and I to figure out our future prospects. They were both tired of London, and suggested rather casually one evening that we should consider emigrating to Canada. Why not? When you are 22 years of age with an enquiring sense of adventure, then the prospect of a new world is very enticing.

I must say that we did not give this suggestion much consideration. I do not recall any deep and meaningful discussions on the subject, beyond a general acclamation that it sounded like a good idea, and that we should make some enquiries. It is interesting to note how little consideration we gave to this rather momentous decision, given what an enormous impact this move would have on our futures.

Canada Maybe.

Toronto seemed to be the best option as it was a young and vibrant city, was English speaking, and presented the best job opportunities. I wrote to various hotels seeking employment and received a positive reply from the general manager of the Inn On The Park hotel, advising me that they were impressed with my background, and could offer me a position on reception, if and when I secured my visa. My two mates did not bother to enquire, and decided to take their chances after arrival in Canada.

We submitted our applications for immigration to the Canadian High Commission in London. Some weeks later we were invited to attend interviews. This was very encouraging. On the appointed day, we turned up at Canada House and were directed to the interview rooms. My two colleagues were interviewed by the same immigration official, and I was interviewed by a separate official. I must say that I did not feel very confident, as the official I was dealing with seemed to adopt the attitude that the hotel industry in Toronto was in its infancy, and that I had very limited job prospects. This was despite my letter of offer from the Inn on the Park.

On the other hand, my two friends were absolutely delighted as the official virtually handed them visas on the spot. And this was the result. My colleagues received letters of confirmation including immigration visas and I was refused due to my limited job prospects. I had a job offer while my two friends had not even bothered to make enquiries, and I was rejected and they were approved. We all three had similar backgrounds, same age, work experience, and all were in good health. I was the only one with a job offer but I am the one who is refused a visa. It did not seem fair!

So, I decided to appeal the decision. I wrote a polite letter to the Canadian Ambassador suggesting that I had been unfairly treated, was very keen to emigrate to his great country, and would appreciate some further consideration. Low and behold I received a reply inviting me for a second interview.

On the second occasion I was interviewed by the same official who had interviewed my friends. This delightful gentleman chatted with me for a while, smiled, shook my hand and said 'welcome to Canada'. And in jest he said, 'if ever I am in Toronto and can't find a hotel room I hope you will remember me'. I assured him that I certainly would.

I must say that this official understood and enacted the policy of his government in selecting individuals for immigration. Young, fit, and well educated individuals make significant contributions to any society, and the Canadian government was keen to identify and attract immigrants of this nature. My previous interviewer simply had a closed mind, and if I had accepted his decision I would not have had the opportunity to prosper in that wonderful country. Government bureaucrats are often guilty of such ineptitude, and must surely have thwarted the dreams of many prospective and appropriate immigrants.

Visit Home.

We arranged to travel home to Ireland to say farewell to our families. Billy and I decided to take the Morris Oxford on the ferry, while Jim travelled separately. We arranged to meet up at Shannon airport some weeks later for the flight to Toronto.

We drove to Liverpool and made our way to the car ferry for the overnight trip to Dublin. While parking the car it struck me that there were a significant number of rather large trucks on board. However, I did not notice the significance of our parking spot relative to the trucks. We set sail for Dublin, had dinner and the obligatory few pints in the bar. This was the beginning of quite a significant journey in our lives, and called for some celebration.

We retired to bed quite late and did not hear, or pay attention to, the early morning announcement seeking the owners of a car registration number. The ferry had stopped, and we presumed we were in Dublin. Eventually, however, it dawned on me that the registration number in the now urgent announcements was ours.

We packed our belongings and rushed to the car deck, where we realised that our car was blocking the exit of the trucks onto the docks, and the truck drivers were very angry. We were almost physically assaulted by these burly drivers, and certainly endured a very rude verbal attack with one driver yelling 'move this piece of shit or I will push it into the harbour, and you two with it'. Fearing for our safety, we jumped into the car and sped off to Dublin. Obviously, in those days the system of ticket allocation did not link cars with cabins. I assume it changed after our experience.

Billy and I parted company in Dublin. He headed to his home in Tipperary, and me to Monaghan in the Morris Oxford, which I was hoping to dispose of across the border in Northern Ireland, as it was a UK registered vehicle. I could not find a buyer, but after my departure for Canada, my dear father managed to sell the car to a gentleman in Armagh, just across the border, for the sum total of five pounds. We had a lot of fun in that old jalopy!

Toronto

We boarded Aer Lingus at Shannon Airport on November 30th 1970, bound for Canada. How exciting it was arriving in Toronto. People spoke with what I then regarded as American accents, cars were enormous, roadways were wide and spacious. The atmosphere was so refreshing and vibrant. People seemed to be happy and hospitable. It was like being in an American movie. I loved it.

However, our immediate concern was to find a place to stay. We enquired of the taxi driver, who appraised us and figured we did not have a lot of money, so he drove us to the cheapest place in town, The Ford Hotel. This, however, was not an encouraging introduction to Canada. My initial impressions were somewhat dented. The Ford Hotel was a very seedy establishment in a very seedy part of town. A motley collection of strange characters hung around the front door and the lobby. But perhaps they were just the same as us, Immigrant types with little money and scarce job prospects.

We were allocated two rooms, a twin for Billy and I and Jim in the single. However, the hotel corridors were very dark and dreary and quite scary. Jim decided it was not safe in a single room so moved in with us and slept on the couch. It was late when we arrived, so we decided to have an early night in order to start the search for more permanent, and less intimidating accommodation, the following morning.

After a few days hunting down permanent digs we were walking down a street in the Dundas area, and a Yugoslavian fellow hailed us from his front porch asking us if we were looking for rooms. Coincidentally he had just finished renovating his house, and was looking for lodgers. We must have looked like house hunters. He was right!

We inspected the rooms and made a deal. There were two rooms but one had a double bed so Billy and I had to share, but the price was right, and beggars can't be choosers. Jim again managed to secure the single. The following day we moved in, relieved to get out of the Ford Hotel. In fact, some few weeks later, we read that an unfortunate Indian immigrant had fallen to his death down the lift shaft at The Ford. The lift failed to arrive, but the doors opened, and he stepped into the void. Some months later the Ford was closed by order of the council and was later demolished.

Finding jobs now became the priority. I contacted the Inn on the Park hotel and was invited for an interview with the elegant and very British general manager, Stuart Covington. Being British, Covington was aware of Grosvenor House and immediately offered me a job on reception, or front desk, as it is referred to in America. The Inn on the Park had been developed by the real estate entrepreneur, Issy Sharp, and was the precursor to the world renowned Four Seasons hotel company, also developed by Sharpe. It was a beautiful property situated in its own grounds at Don Mills, just on the edge of the city.

Jim managed to secure employment in a hotel on the lake shore, but even then I could see that his interest in being a hotelier was waning. However, as mentioned previously, he would go on to greater things, developing the highly successful Rundles Restaurant in Startford which he owned for 40 years.

Billy also got a job at the Inn on the Park. This was the rather unlikely position of Timekeeper. Unlikely because our social lives were not conducive to Billy rising each morning at 4.30am, for a starting time of 6am, which I figured would be a challenge. Those days employees were required to enter the hotel through a dedicated entrance where they punched a time card, which recorded their hours of work. The Timekeeper manned the entranceway from a little cubicle, and monitored employee comings and goings, as well as issuing time cards.

So we were now all gainfully employed and about to experience our first Canadian winter. The first snowfall that year occurred on December 1, the day after our arrival. We were not really equipped for the sudden fall in temperature, as we had discarded what had become shabby winter overcoats prior to departing London.

On walking down Yonge St one day, the icy cold drove us into an army disposal store, which we exited rugged up in heavy coats and beanies. Adjusting to winter time in Toronto took some doing. Ireland can experience cold winters, but nothing compared to the chill felt in Canada. On some occasions, the weather man would forecast the temperature at minus 20, but with a wind chill which took it down to minus 40. That is cold!

We settled down quite quickly in Toronto and, despite the cold of our first winter, we were generally very enthusiastic about our new surroundings. Canada is a great and very civilised country, and Canadians are generally very nice people. At that time, Toronto was home to thousands of immigrants from almost every nation on earth. Over 50 per cent of the population was under the age of 30, most of them immigrants.

It was heartening to observe how the immigrants identified with their new home. In most pubs that rousing national anthem, Oh Canada, was played at the end of each evening, and immigrants stood as one and sang heartily. This, I felt, was a great achievement for a new country which very obviously managed, not only to integrate its immigrant population, but made them feel proud and happy to be there. Many other nations could and should learn the Canadian way.

As expected, Billy's time keeping job presented challenges. Using tram and bus it took almost one hour to travel to the Inn on the Park. That meant a 4.30 am wake up before departing at 5am for a 6am start. Needless to say, and due to our late night frolics, my timekeeper mate with whom I was sharing a double bed, missed his wakeup from time to time. This caused his boss to scold him and threaten his employment.

In desperation, Billy took to setting his alarm clock and positioning a box of matches on his night table. Turning in at say, midnight, I would be awakened by Billy striking a match to check the clock. Only 1.30am. Back to sleep to be awoken again by the match striking at 3am. Somehow, despite these efforts, he would instinctively turn off the alarm when it rang and go back to sleep.

Then I would be awakened by a loud roar, "oh, Fuck" and Billy would dash to the bathroom, it being 6.30 or beyond. After a number of late arrivals, Billy's boss, who was very fond of him, decided that the only way to get him to work on time was for he, the boss, to pick him up in the mornings. This worked, but there were occasions when the boss was left banging on the front door in an attempt to waken Billy. This of course also woke our Yugoslavian landlord, who was none too pleased.

The time keeping job was simply not appropriate to Billy's personality, and was certainly well below his level of competence. He took on a position in the beverage industry working for Gilbeys, a large distributor of wines and spirits. This was obviously his calling, for some years later he was to become recognised as one of Canada's leading wine experts and writers, publishing very popular newsletters and wine books.

On the Front Desk

I enjoyed working at the Inn on the Park and became team leader on the front desk. That meant that I was responsible for allocating the rooms for all the incoming guests. The hotel rooms were located on both sides of the building, one side overlooking the pool and the other with views of the city, or to be more precise, the railway track. Obviously, customers who knew the hotel requested the pool view. But with the rooms roughly divided 50 per cent, half the customers were going to be allocated with views of the rail track.

This was the cause of huge fights on reception. Every weekend the hotel was fully booked from Friday to Sunday with visiting Americans from across the border. Friday was therefore the day of battle stations for the reception staff. Almost every reservation would feature a request for pool views, and half of them were going to be disappointed. The hotel reservations department always advised customers that their request for a particular view was noted, but not guaranteed.

However, the regular customers knew that some were going to be the lucky ones, and some not so lucky. This led to endless confrontations on check in once the customer was informed that they were on the city side of the hotel, or, as the customer would retort, the railway track view.

Being the person responsible for room allocations, the customers would request to speak with me directly and demand a poolside room. Obviously, I could not change the allocation for one customer, as many of them knew each other and would immediately advise their friends that they had secured a pool view room. This would cause uproar among those with whom we had already dealt, and who were unsuccessful in securing a change of room.

On some occasions the customers became so belligerent and threatening that I had to advise them that the hotel was fully booked and had a waitlist, and if they did not want the room that was allocated, I could easily sell it to another customer. This seemed to do the trick, and the customer would walk off in a huff threatening to report me to senior management for my rude and uncooperative approach. Senior management were all too aware of the situation and tended not to get involved. Obviously, this dilemma could have been easily solved by imposing a surcharge for pool rooms, but management was not so enlightened in those days!

The Inn on the Park was the host hotel in 1971 for the visit of Alexei Kosygin, the Premier of the USSR. The hotel was chosen because of its location in its own grounds on the city outskirts. The RCMP considered it easier to provide security than for a city centre hotel. In fact, the hotel was simply ringed by armed federal officers standing approximately 10 metres apart for 24 hours of each day. It was quite a forbidding sight as one approached the hotel, with every staff member and customer being frisked on arrival.

On one occasion, I was asked to deliver an invitation to the suite of Mr Kosygin. I duly took the elevator to the penthouse floor, being somewhat surprised that I was not challenged prior to entering the elevator. However, on alighting on the designated floor, I was confronted by federal agents with drawn guns, who challenged my presence on the floor. I was in a hotel uniform, and I nervously advised these agents that I was delivering an invitation for Mr Kosygin from the Mayor of Toronto. I was relieved of the envelope, and advised to withdraw from the floor.

Obviously, something had gone terribly wrong with the surveillance team communication system. Whoever was meant to be screening people entering the elevators was either not on the ball or distracted. Whatever the reason, I think this incident demonstrates how a nervous and armed police official could over react and injure an innocent person going about their work. It was quite a scary experience.

Rules of the Road

We decided to move house and secured a very nice arrangement on the top floor of a duplex in Highbourne road. There were two large bedrooms, a living room and a rather extensive dining room, not to mention an eat in kitchen. We decided that we would not require the use of the dining room, and could sublet it as bedroom accommodation to two of our college friends whom we had come across unexpectedly.

Eoin Kennedy was employed by the Irish Tourist Board in Toronto, and Michael Bewley had just secured a job on reception at the Inn on the Park. Mike was one of the illustrious Bewley family who had established and owned the famous Bewleys Café in Grafton St in Dublin. So Eoin and Mike became lodgers and gladly shared the dining room where we had provided appropriate bedding. The duplex was large enough for all of us, and we were generally congenial company for each other.

Eoin was the owner of a Ford Mustang which was pretty cool. He generously offered it to me so that I could get some practice driving on the other side of the road, so to speak. On one occasion I had taken the Mustang for a ride and had turned right on a red signal believing this to be the rule, as long as it was safe to do so.

I was stopped by a cop who advised me that I had contravened the law by not coming to a full stop before turning. I advised him that I was not long in Toronto, had applied for a Canadian licence, and was seeking to become comfortable with driving on the right, and within the local laws. He was pleasant, said he understood, and wished me well. However, a few weeks later I received a fine in the mail. This disappointed me considerably and I decided to contest the fine in court.

On the appointed day I turned up at the Toronto court of petty sessions to be confronted by a courtroom full of appellants, all pleading not guilty for a myriad of traffic offences. People fined for driving too slowly on a highway, cars overloaded with goods and people, failing to stop at stop signs, and so on. I observed the proceedings and noticed that each person, when asked by the very bored magistrate, pleaded not guilty. Then a long winding story would unfold to justify the misdemeanour, as the magistrate almost fell asleep with the boredom of yet another sorry tale. Each and every story ended with the magistrate banging his gavel and pronouncing guilty!

My turn came and I was asked how I wished to plead. 'Guilty, I said, 'with extenuating circumstance'. This got the magistrate's attention. 'Tell me about the extenuating circumstance', he said. I told him that I had not been in the country very long, that I had misunderstood the rule but that I had not caused any damage, and since the incident, I had completed my driving test and was now entirely aware of the rules. I was delighted to hear the magistrate say ' Case dismissed'.

An Aussie Nurse.

Mike was friendly with some nurses who worked at the Mount Sinai hospital. He invited a group of these lovely ladies to visit us for drinks at Highbourne Road. One of these nurses was a lovely Australian, with the intriguing Irish name of Cathie Murphy. I was immediately smitten by this lovely lady. She was outgoing, personable, and simply smashing. And she had the cutest voice and accent.

We fell into a very deep and meaningful conversation, about which I do not recall one iota. But we seemed to hit if off immediately, and enjoyed our short time chatting. I was quite enraptured, and made plans to meet again as soon as possible.

An opportunity arose with the Inn on the Park staff party, which was to be held on a boat on lake Ontario. I contacted

Cathie and shyly told her that a group of us was going to the party and invited her to join us. I say shyly because I was not specific in asking her to join me, but to join our group. At least this is how she understood the invitation. She asked if she could bring a friend and I said certainly, assuming it would be one of her nursing mates.

To my great regret and surprise, she brought a male friend, which cramped my style somewhat. My fellow party goers, Billy, Jim and Mike, being aware of my feelings, found the situation very amusing. So my first sortie with this beautiful lady proved less than encouraging.

However, fortune favours the brave, so I soldiered on and invited Cathie to a friend's party which was to be held some distance outside the city. I was the owner at that time of a rather dodgy and ancient Triumph Herald. I arranged to pick Cathie up at her residence in the company of Jim and his friend Marie.

I escorted Cathie to the car and gallantly opened the door for her. Then I proceeded to open the driver's door, but the damn thing was stuck, and after wrestling with it for some time I decided that my only option was to climb in the window. What a start! In any case, off we went to the party and had a nice time.

However, more disaster was in store on the way home. The car started to overheat with steam erupting from the bonnet. I stopped and went searching for water by the roadside, using an empty beer bottle to gather what I could from the ditch. This was the procedure all the way back to Toronto, with weird sounds and more steam resulting in frequent stops for more water. What a disaster. My companions, including Cathie, laughed heartily, but I wondered what impression I was making on the fair Aussie.

Not so good, I thought, but I was wrong. Despite these rather dubious starts, Cathie and I were married in Toronto on June 23, 1973, which, at the time of writing, is exactly 46 years ago. And we have had a very full life together. Certainly never boring, as she often says!

Mind you, we almost had a missed opportunity during the courting period! Cathie had always planned to tour Europe, so she was rightly determined to stick to her plan. We agreed that she would go off on her travels, and that we would meet at Dublin airport on a specific time and date some three months hence. This would be a test of our relationship. Should one of us choose not to turn up then that would be a signal that it was nice knowing you, so to speak, but we should go our separate ways!

I duly arrived in Dublin somewhat apprehensive and hoping Cathie would make the rendezvous. However, there was no sign of her when I arrived. So, I decided to wait for a number of flights from Europe, hoping she would be on one. After a few hours I decided that she had had a change of heart and was not going to appear.

So, somewhat disappointed, I made my way onward to Monaghan to visit my parents, who I had previously alerted to the possibility of a young lady accompanying me. Of course, I had to explain to them what had occurred and made a brave effort at a c'est le vie attitude.

The next day, my father, who was a complete golf fanatic, arranged for us to have a game at his local club. We duly set off in the morning and had a nice time at Rossmore Golf club, distracted as I was over the Aussie nurse! On arriving back at my parent's house, I noticed my sister's car parked outside, and was conscious on entering the house of a number of people chatting in the living room. I imagined it was my sister, husband and kids coming to say hello. What a shock had I on entering the room.

There, in the midst of my family, and not understanding a word they were saying, sat the beautiful Cathie. Wow, what a great surprise! But I needed to know what happened and how did she find firstly, Monaghan, and then my family? Her plane was delayed, and on not finding me at the airport she decided to enquire on how to get to Monaghan. She was advised to take the express bus, which took approximately two hours. However, she did not arrive in Monaghan until the evening, so decided to stay in a bed and breakfast and to enquire about the whereabouts of the Holland family in the morning.

Unfortunately, as luck would have it, the owners of the B&B were new to the town and did not, of course, know anything of the Hollands. However, not to be outdone, Cathie, thinking that Monaghan is a relatively small town, wondered if the telephone operator would know the Hollands. This worked, as the operator was actually a friend of my sister, Nora, and immediately put Cathie through.

My sister was simply mortified! That a young Australian girl would come all that way and be left to spend the night in a B&B was embarrassing, to say the least. Nora duly drove to the B&B and brought Cathie to our home in Old Cross Square. I, of course, was delighted, despite my sister's embarrassment.

Sherwood Avenue

Back in Toronto, my mates and I moved house again! This time we decided to rent a three storey on Sherwood Avenue. One significant and attractive feature was the fact that the house had a bar in the basement. The previous occupants were Irish tradesmen who had actually decided to build a boat in the basement. Unfortunately, when the boat was complete they found that it would not fit out the door. A boat in a basement is not much use to anyone, so our erstwhile tradies dismantled it, and used the wood to build a bar. Yes, from time to time we Irish are delightfully silly!

St Patrick's Day Parade

Many cities in North America had a St Patricks Day parade, but not Toronto, despite a huge preponderance of Irish immigrants and many Canadians with Irish heritage. The city had been what was referred to as WASP, that is White Anglo Saxon Protestant, for many generations. That, perhaps, was why there was no St Patrick's Day parade.

So, we decided to right this terrible wrong. Billy Munnelly, Kevin Leahy, a dear departed friend, and I decorated Leahy's Pontiac convertible automobile with shamrocks, bunting and all things Irish, and proceeded to drive down Toronto's

Yonge St waving to the populace. It was amazing how many people waved back at us, and some even cheered.

Our one vehicle motorcade continued all the way down to Front Street on Lake Ontario, where we went in search of a pub. Low and behold, we found a pub that was festooned in green, with patrons celebrating their Irishness. It was almost like a secret society! We were welcomed and feted. We featured on the nightly television news, with a comment from the Lord Mayor that it would be appropriate for Toronto to have an official St Patricks Day parade. So, we lay claim to being the inaugurators of what is now quite a huge annual event. Big things have small beginnings.

Entering the World of Hyatt

The Front Office Manager at the Inn on the Park was a Turkish gentleman by the name of Cafir Iz. He and I became quite friendly and seemed to have a mutually balanced view of the world. He had a good sense of humour, and seemed to appreciate my unorthodox Irish slant on things. He introduced me to a person who was going to have a significant effect on my future career, both positive and negative.

Andre Pury was the newly appointed Front Office Manager of the Hyatt Regency Toronto, a luxury hotel being developed on Avenue Road and Bloor, in the then bohemian suburb of Yorkville. I had heard about the opening of the Hyatt, but was not particularly aware of the Hyatt brand, as it was, at that time, US based, with Toronto being one of the company's early initiatives in the international market.

Hyatt was and is owned by the Pritzker family of Chicago. This family was very successful in a number of industries, but had no interest in the hotel business until one of the sons, Jay Pritzker, happened to stay at a Los Angeles airport motel which was up for sale. The name of the motel was the Hyatt House named after its owner, Hyatt Von Dehn.

Pritzker made enquiries and ended up purchasing the motel in 1957 for approximately $2 million. He and his family then went on to develop other airport located motels until he was presented the opportunity of purchasing a hotel under development in Atlanta, where the developers had gone into bankruptcy. He acquired the hotel, completed it, and was surprised to realise that there was a much greater return in the luxury end of the market than in motels.

The Hyatt Regency Atlanta, incidentally, was the first hotel in the world to feature an atrium lobby. This investment encouraged Pritzker to divest of the motels, and to concentrate in the upper end of the market. He opened a number of U.S. properties, before taking his first step internationally with the takeover of the President Hotel in Hong Kong in 1969, to be renamed the Hyatt Regency Hong Kong. Other international developments followed, including Toronto.

I met Andre Pury and he offered me the position of Assistant Manager, Front Office. This was quite exciting and I enthusiastically accepted his offer. I had enjoyed my time at the Inn on the Park, and often wonder where I would have ended up had I stayed with Four Seasons. But I was not to know of the outstanding success that company would achieve in the future. Mind you, Hyatt also achieved wonderful success, so no point in thinking of what might have been, except to say that I think Four Seasons was more the luxury brand and style that I enjoyed most.

The opening of the Hyatt Regency in Toronto was greatly anticipated. Toronto was short of quality hotels and the introduction of this luxury product, conveniently located at Avenue Rd and Bloor, suggested a successful venture. The hotel featured 400 rooms and suites, a number of fine restaurants, and an array of conference facilities.

It also featured what could only be described as an oddity! The licensing laws at that time were a throwback from the days of the city being WASP, which I have explained previously. It was forbidden to stand in a bar, carry your glass of alcohol from one table to another and to drink alcohol in your back garden unless your hedges were high enough, so that neighbours would not be offended by the sight of people drinking!

In this environment the Hyatt applied for and was given a licence to allow 21 people standing in the bar, which was known as the SRO, or Standing Room Only Bar. This was the only bar in Toronto where drinkers could actually stand at the bar. And as a result of this novelty, there was a continuous line up to enter the bar when the hotel opened.

The bar manager had to actually count the number standing in case he fell afoul of the police Morality Squad. Yes, that was the title of this particular police squad, whose role was to monitor the behaviour of licensees. They often came to the hotel and counted the number of standing drinkers, requiring the manager to remove a patron to the top of the queue, if there was one more than the limit.

The hotel General Manager was the illustrious Franz Schutzman. He was a very colourful, sophisticated and charming individual. Born in the Dutch East Indies he had worked and lived all over the world, with suggestions that he had been a spy for the allies in Italy during the Second World War. He spoke English, Dutch, German, French and Italian fluently. He had previously opened and operated the Cavalieri Hilton in Rome, and the Nile Hilton in Cairo. He was a stickler for guest service and could become totally unreasonable if a customer reported any deficiency in service.

In fact, his lovely secretary, Elaine, would warn department managers that Schutzman had received a guest complaint, and it would be best if that particular manager made themselves scarce for the rest of the day. Or as Elaine would say, it is probably best if you are not here today for if Mr Schutzman sees you, you may not be here tomorrow, or any other day! The next day, Schutzman would have calmed down, and would then gently impress on the particular department manager that he or she must do better.

The hotel opened to great fanfare and was a roaring success from day one. In fact, it ran an occupancy of 90 percent in the first year of operation. My role was to supervise the reception operation and to act as duty manager on occasions. I was assisted by two colleagues and we rotated the various shifts, assisting with check ins and check outs, dealing with guest issues, and managing the room inventory to ensure maximum occupancy.

We were also charged with monitoring the credit worthiness of incoming customers. This particular duty was carried out by examining each and every registration card and ensuring that the customer had provided genuine information, such as an address, and or company affiliation. The easiest way to check an address was by calling the long distance operator and asking for a listing at the address given on the registration card. If the response was 'no listing' then alarm bells would ring as to the integrity of the registration details and, more importantly, the credit worthiness of the individual concerned.

It may sound incredible, but there have always been people who attempt to register and stay at luxury hotels under false names. In those days the use of credit cards was not as common as today, so it was not always possible to secure incoming customers credit details. In fact, some very worthy individuals used to take exception to being required to produce credit identification, as they simply did not use credit cards. In these instances, confirming a listing with the telephone operator gave some comfort to the hotel that the person involved was genuine, and was not using a false name.

However, frequently, a suspicious reception manager would refuse entry to a client after determining that a false address had been registered. In such cases the client involved would be asked to pay cash in advance, and if they refused to do so, would not be admitted to the hotel. One took some pleasure from confronting such individuals who often tore up the registration card and threw it at the manager. Caught you!

However, on one memorable occasion a bogus registration card slipped the net, and had not been picked up by the manager on duty. This came to light when I was called by the housekeeping supervisor to report that a guest in a certain suite had attempted to molest one of the cleaning staff. I immediately checked the customer's registration details, who had registered under the name of White. I received the not so comforting report from the operator of 'no listing'. Obviously, we had a customer using a false address. I then checked the account and noticed that the total was approximately $1500 made up almost entirely of alcohol ordered through room service. This looked like a very dodgy client indeed.

I contacted my boss, Andre Pury, and advised him of the situation. We decided to visit the client in his suite to firstly enquire about his accosting of the cleaning lady, and secondly, the matter of the bogus address, and the extraordinary account which he had charged. We knocked on the door of the suite which was opened by a quite inebriated gentleman, unshaven, wearing a long night shirt. The time was early afternoon.

We asked if we could come in and speak to him about some issues. He threw the door back and waved us in, where we confronted him about the molestation report. He roared laughing, and made some disparaging remarks about the maid, who he maintained he was attempting to have come and clean up his room. 'Look at the mess', said he. And he was right, the room was indeed a mess with empty liquor bottles strewn on the floor, and the remains of half eaten food on dishes, also on the floor. "This is a disgrace" he said, and we should be ashamed of such poor service. We acknowledged that the room certainly did require servicing, and that we would arrange to have this done.

However, we broached the subject of his outstanding account, and suggested that he should settle it, or produce some credit identification to support the expenses incurred. Again, he laughed and fell back on his bed, resulting in his night shirt rolling up exposing his genitalia. This was not a pleasant sight. He said 'where the hell do you think I am going to find $1500 on a Saturday'. There were no ATMs those days! He found the whole scenario very amusing and laughed again.

By this stage he was referring to me as Paddy, and to Andre as 'the Greek', due to his European colouring. He then decided to make a long distance phone call and spoke to someone with whom he was very familiar. He was very jolly and seemed to find the whole situation hilarious. He told his telephone acquaintance that he was at the Hyatt in Toronto, was obviously under the influence, and that he had two 'bastards' in his room demanding money. He hung up and said ' just you wait'.

Almost immediately the phone rang, and he said that the call was for me. I answered, and was confronted by a very sophisticated and angry voice asking my name and position. I was then told that I was disturbing a very illustrious person and that if I valued my job, I should withdraw from the room immediately and leave Mr White alone. The caller warned me again and hung up. Mr White again roared laughing, and told me that I should heed the advice I had just received.

By this stage both Andre and I were warming to Mr White. He was obviously intelligent, sophisticated, and apart from the night shirt, his other clothes which we observed, were of excellent quality. His predicament was amusing, to him and to us. However, we needed some comfort regarding the bill. Low and behold, Mr White reluctantly presented us with a Canadian Pacific Airlines credit card, in a company name. Those days such a card could also be used for expenses, other than airline travel. We processed the card and were surprised that the charges were approved. We added some additional funds to the amount outstanding to cover any further expenses which might be incurred, but we cut the supply of alcohol.

The next day, Mr White checked out. By then the story had spread around the hotel and the bar manager, Stan Kozak, who was an old hand in the Toronto hotel scene, asked me if the guest in question had used the name of White. Indeed he did, I replied. Well, he said, that gentleman is the leading stock broker in Canada, and every so often the pressure becomes too much, and he checks into a hotel under an assumed name, spending the weekend on an alcoholic bender. He will be back, he said.

Some six months later when I had become Front Office Manager, one of the reception staff came to my office to tell me that there was an inebriated gentleman at reception asking for the Irishman or the Greek. On seeing me, Mr White roared with his infectious laugh, and I instructed the reception to check him in, and I escorted him to his suite. I heard nothing of his activity over the weekend, but I had warned the housekeeping department to make sure his room was properly serviced.

The Teamsters Union.

The hotel subscribed to an agreement with the notorious Teamsters Union, based in Chicago, but with coverage in Toronto. This was somewhat of a formality, as the employees were generally well looked after, and seemed happy. However, on one occasion the doorman, whose job it was to control traffic in the driveway and to valet park customers cars, actually crashed a customer's car, causing significant damage. It was evident that the doorman in question was somewhat inebriated at the time, and he was consequently sacked.

He appealed to the Teamsters, who dispatched two of their executives from Chicago to investigate the case. I was immediately struck by the appearance of these two individuals with their camel hair overcoats and fedora hats. Very much in the style of the mob, I thought. However, these were street smart individuals.

They interviewed the doorman and the supervisor who was on duty. They enquired of the doorman as to how much money he made each week. The doorman quoted his union wage which was approximately $150 per week. We know your weekly wage, they said, but what we want to know is how much money you take home every week from tips. The doorman responded that on a normal week he took home $900. In 1972 it was not a bad take home pay. The Teamsters looked at him and said, 'If you are so stupid as to jeopardise a job that pays you that much, don't bother us. You deserve to be fired'. Matter closed. Now that's a smart and pragmatic union.

Wedding Bells

On return from Ireland, Cathie and I moved into a duplex on Sherwood Avenue, which Billy, Jim and I had managed to purchase. Billy had secured a loan with draconian interest rates from a Jewish money lender, by the name of Moses Lazarus. Cathie and I paid rent. This was a very pleasant arrangement and we enjoyed living together. In a very short time, I broached the subject of marriage, a proposal duly accepted.

We were married at the Franciscan Friary on Avenue Road. Billy was my Best Man and Jim was Grooms Man. The reception was held in the Penthouse Suite of the Hyatt Regency, with the compliments of Franz Schutzman. We did not see a bill, which was a wonderful gesture on the part of Schutzman. Cathie's mother came all the way from Australia for the occasion.

We honeymooned in Spain and Ireland. My family in Monaghan gave us a second reception at the Westenra hotel, which was a lovely and memorable occasion.

Bali

Andre Pury had been transferred to a place called Bali, to open the Bali Hyatt. I had never heard of Bali at that time, but I wished Andre well and I replaced him as Front Office Manager. However, a short time later, I received a message from Andre asking me if I would care to join him in Bali as Front Office Manager, to open the hotel. As I have said, I did not know anything about Bali but Cathie informed me that it was located close to Australia. This all sounded very exciting, and Cathie had not been back to Australia for six years, so she was quite keen on the idea. She also had difficulty with the Canadian winters, and found the cold of Toronto very uncomfortable. We made the decision to explore the idea and I duly informed Andre of my interest.

I can vividly remember the sense of adventure I felt on the prospects of heading off to Asia. I was a bit apprehensive, of course, but found the whole proposition quite intriguing. One apprehension was to do with all the inoculations we were required to have before departure. Yellow Fever, Tetanus, Diphtheria, and Typhoid warnings did not fill one with great comfort about the environment in which we would be living. Medical facilities were also pretty doubtful, I was advised.

We travelled from Toronto to San Francisco and onward to Singapore with Philippine Airlines via Manila. I thought the journey would never end! However, Singapore was an extraordinary experience for one who had never been to Asia. And this was 1973, long before the era of skyscrapers and casinos. We stayed at the Hyatt Regency Singapore, and spent wondrous days exploring the city, as we waited for our visas to travel to Bali.

Flights to Bali were infrequent those days. Thai International provided two flights each week, and Pan Am had a once weekly flight from Hong Kong. Garuda of course flew to Bali, but via Jakarta. We arrived at Denpasar airport on Thai International to be met by Andre, and the General Manager of the Bali Hyatt, Marc Hamel. My first impression was of an island covered in rice fields and palm trees. There was very little development in what was then an island paradise.

We were deposited in a very simple Losmen, or bed and breakfast hostel. This was located on Sanur Beach, not far from the iconic Tanjung Sari hotel, where we were provided with most of our meals. Our first experience of Bali cuisine, however, was breakfast in the Losmen. This was an interesting experience as none of the staff spoke any English, and we of course did not speak Bahasa Indonesian.

With no experience of the East, we tended to search for our regular breakfast items like toast and cereal. I recall that we could not communicate the meaning of toast, and received warmed up bread wrapped in a napkin, every morning. Looking back, it is sad how unadventurous we were in that it was quite a few months before we started to experience the local cuisine. Many tourists are like that today, and miss out on some wonderful culinary experiences as a result.

The Bali Hyatt was also located on Sanur Beach. It is hard to believe that this was to be only the second international hotel on the island, the original being the Bali Beach, which was built by the Japanese as war reparation! It was quite idyllic to stroll along the beach to work each morning. The local people were delightful, with cheerful greetings and no hawking of paraphernalia, as is the case today. Most were fishermen and farmers, and a few who worked in hospitality.

This was the Bali beloved of the generation of hippies who traversed the globe. Bali was on the main route between Europe and Sydney, and many of the beautiful people stopped off en route in either direction. Some stayed a few days, but in most cases they got lost in smoking grass or eating magic mushrooms at Kuta Beach and tended to stay until their money ran out. Kuta Beach was famous for its sunsets, and was totally undeveloped. This was Nirvana where everything was cheap, the weather balmy, and days were whiled away in a state of contentment. It is no longer like that, unfortunately, with the area now desecrated with night clubs, discos and massage parlours.

The Bali Hyatt

The Bali Hyatt was under construction. It was owned by two Texas oil men who had allocated $8 million to purchase the land, build and equip the hotel, and pay wages until the opening. This was simply not enough money to do the job, given that the hotel had almost 400 rooms. However, the two Texans were determined not to contribute one extra cent, despite much pleading from Hyatt. As a result, the opening was done on a shoe string budget. Andre Pury even resorted to providing the hotel office stationery by using stencilled forms with carbon paper, stapled together. We could not afford to have them printed.

The management team was somewhat top heavy with expatriates, and that factor put extra pressure on the budget. The General Manager, Marc Hamel, was a French Canadian, Andre and the Food and Beverage Manager, Arthur Holliger, Swiss, the Head Chef George and one of his assistants, Claude, French, the other Assistant Chef, Freddie, German, the Housekeeper Miss Jeffrey, English, the Chief Engineer, Kamnung, Thai, the Financial Controller, Edmund Ip, Hong

Kong Chinese, a Purchasing Administrator, Neal Locke, American, and a logistics administrator who was German. Then myself, an Irishman. With the exception of Edmund from Hong Kong and Kamnung from Thailand, not one of these managers ever had any previous experience in Asia. Our lack of experience did cause some significant challenges, especially given the somewhat corrupt regime which ruled Indonesia those days.

We were babes in the wood, so to speak. Or perhaps more like bulls in a china shop. Most of us were in our twenties, and were totally uninformed in terms of the culture and traditions of the Balinese. Some brashness and insensitivity was evident, but with time we learned to love and respect these beautiful people, and their spiritual and colourful traditions.

As the opening date approached, we were presented with some interesting dilemmas. One had to do with a shipment of wine for the restaurants. The Purchasing Manager approached the General Manager advising him that he was about to clear the wine through customs. He indicated that in order to achieve a smooth transaction, certain funds would need to be provided to the customs officers. The General Manager was a rather straight laced individual, who practically threw the purchasing manager out of his office for suggesting that he, the GM, approve bribery. We never did receive the wine shipment.

The same thing occurred with the first shipment of very expensive US beef. Customs, who by this stage knew the Bali Hyatt was a non payer, decided to cause as much obstruction as possible. We received a call to advise us that our shipment of beef was on the tarmac, and should be urgently cleared. However, since we were not paying the appropriate fee, the beef was not cleared and was left to rot.

This situation continued with almost every item we attempted to import. Officialdom in Indonesia lived on the proceeds of bribes, and any organisation wishing to do business had to cooperate, or fail.

This principle applied even to the Immigration officials on the island. The Chief of Immigration actually became friendly with the hotel management and we often entertained him to drinks. On one occasion we decided to ask him why we, expatriates, paid significantly more for an exit visa than a local. The Immigration Chief frankly advised us that his budget for running his office covered only two employees, although he required 20 to do the job. 'Where do you think I can get the additional funds', he asked. 'You expatriates do not pay tax', he said, 'so why don't you just treat the additional charge as taxation'. Very frank, indeed.

A young Australian engineer, with whom we played tennis, also had an interesting experience when attempting to deliver Australian aid to Bali in the form of a network of water pipes, necessary to provide clean drinking water to some villages. Having only been in Bali for a few months, he went to the airport to clear a delivery of water pipes for the aid work.

The customs advised him that he would have to pay a duty fee of 20,000 rupiah, to which he reacted rather abruptly, stating that he did not pay duty on what was essentially a gift from Australia to the people of Indonesia. The customs officer listened to his story and then advised him that if he was not going to pay duty, then he had to complete some forms, to which the engineer agreed. However, the customs official advised him that there were 10 forms costing 2000 rupiah each. In other words, the original "duty" as mentioned.

The engineer refused, and stormed out of the customs office to report the incident to the Australian Embassy in Jakarta. A few days later he was visited by an embassy official who had arranged to have the shipment of pipes cleared. However, the official gave the young engineer some practical advice. 'Our country is attempting to do some outstanding work providing water to the people of Bali', the official said. 'We can only succeed with the cooperation of the island officials, including the customs. The attitude we take is that in order to get the water to the people, we have to be pragmatic. The duty demanded by the corrupt officials is minuscule compared to the total aid project. Rather than deny the people the clean water, are we not better to pay the fee and thereby succeed for the greater good?'

The engineer heeded this lesson and got on with the job. Not many months later, the villages involved were enjoying clean drinking water with children and adults no longer exposed to diseases found in the contaminated water, which they had been using. Not everyone would agree with this approach, but I personally believe that one must play by the rules of the society where one is working.

This very principle was borne out prior to the opening of the hotel when the General Manager was transferred, and was replaced with an individual who had significant experience in Asia. Pierre Bonard was his name, another Swiss. Pierre was a very kind, friendly and engaging individual. He was also very pragmatic when it came to managing the project and dealing with officials. He 'cooperated' with the customs and immediately all shipments to the Bali Hyatt were processed without any obstruction.

However, the officials were always on the lookout for an opportunity to generate some extra income. In this regard, we were contacted by the island telephone chief executive, who said that the telephone installation at the Bali Hyatt was causing disruption to the island telephone services and, if this continued, the hotel telephone service would be disconnected. This was utter nonsense, but we played along professing an apology for our interference. How can we amend the situation, we enquired. By having a telephone company technician located on the hotel switchboard observing the hotel operators, and ensuring that they were not in any way sabotaging the system, we were advised.

This we agreed to, expecting a qualified engineer of some sort. However, the observer was a young trainee who simply sat at the switchboard each day reading magazines and chatting to the operators. The hotel paid a monthly fee for the services of this individual, of course, but the amount was significantly more than the telephone trainee was paid. But our telephone service continued uninterrupted and no further interference was caused to the island network! Everybody was happy!

The Balinese people were absolutely delightful. They are a very spiritual people, and devout Hindus. In those days they lived quite an simple existence in an island paradise. They were self sufficient for food, entirely family orientated, and not yet contaminated by Western culture, except perhaps those who had been blighted by becoming government officials!

Religious festivals seemed to dominate their lives and they were forever leaving little offerings to the gods around the place, in the form of fruit or flowers. In fact, the people believed that the site of the Bali Hyatt was a holy place where the spirits of the dead left the island. This caused significant soul searching on the part of the hotel employees, who refused to start work until the site was blessed by a holy man. This we arranged and after a very pious ceremony in the hotel lobby the staff were happy to start.

Like many expatriate wives, Cathie found that she had too much spare time. After all, there is only so much sun tanning, swimming and ladies lunches one can handle. She decided to conduct English classes for the staff, which were badly needed. These classes were very successful and much appreciated.

She did, however, have one particularly memorable experience that occurred when the Crown Prince of Saudi Arabia came to the hotel on his honeymoon. The happy couple asked to be escorted on a tour of the island, and the art area of Ubud. Cathie offered to be the escort and set off in a chauffeur driven limousine with the royal couple. All went well until the car broke down in the middle of the island, surrounded by rice paddies. With no phones in the area, the driver hitched a ride on a passing motor cycle to go and seek help.

This left Cathie and the Saudi couple sitting on the side of the road. Of course, they were very quickly surrounded by local children who found the tourists very curious, indeed. Despite this rather inconvenient situation, the prince and princess were very relaxed and found the children quite delightful. They laughed and joked and took photos. This experience was hardly up to Hyatt standard, but it surely provided an interesting and memorable tale from their honeymoon. They were rescued by the return of the driver in a more reliable automobile.

The hotel opened in 1973, which was the year of the first international oil crises. The Middle Eastern oil producers imposed an oil embargo on countries which had supported Israel in the Yom Kippur war. This resulted in the oil price going up by over 400 per cent and causing a total disruption to world tourism, and most other industries. Long haul travel collapsed.

As a result, the hotel ran an occupancy of 15 percent in its first year of operation, and this included a period of full occupancy during the traditional Christmas holiday period, when expatriates from mainly Jakarta and Singapore travelled to Bali. There were days when the hotel was literally empty of customers.

This situation made life and work somewhat boring for both employees and management, who simply had little or nothing to do. As a result, the management team sought alternative stimulation by developing a keen interest in the game of tennis. Almost every afternoon the tennis courts were the domain of most of the managers. Competition was fierce and endless and we became, we thought, pretty good players.

The head chef, Fred, and I considered ourselves a formidable doubles team keen to take on all comers. In this regard, it was my role to ensure that any of the few hotel customers who wished to play with us was of an appropriate standard. We did not want to be bothered with hit and giggle types.

On one occasion I had an enquiry from an Australian customer, who had heard that the managers played tennis, and wondered if he could get a game. I rather rudely, as it turned out, enquired about his prowess at the game, seeking to ensure he was up to our standard. He assured me that he was a regular player, so I invited him to join our elite group. This turned out to be quite embarrassing as the individual concerned chose to play with our weakest player against myself and the chef in a doubles match.

He demolished us! We hardly won a single point. After the game, we had a drink and I enquired about this gentleman's tennis background. 'Well, he said, 'I played a lot as a junior and was actually beaten in the Australian Junior Open Final by a chap called Lew Hoad'. Hoad, of course, became World Number One. And here I was casting doubt on this individual's ability. How embarrassing!

I had some very sad news when in Bali. My brother called from Ireland to tell me that my father had died at the tender age of 58 years. He was not a particularly fit individual, but he was a golf fanatic. So much so, that on some days in the summer he would play three rounds of 18 holes. He had been to the doctor about a pain in his chest, which the doctor attributed to a recent bout of flu.

Unfortunately, the doctor was wrong, and my father collapsed and died in the company of my four brothers, playing in the family golf tournament. This was a terrible shock to the whole family of course, and especially my mother. I was so far away that I made the decision not to travel to the funeral, as I thought I would not get there in time. This is a decision I have regretted my whole life, for I could have at least comforted my mother. I have few regrets but this is a big one.

Moving On.

It had always been our intention to travel on to Australia after my period of duty in Bali expired. After a period of two years it was suggested that I explore a role in the Hyatt in Sydney, as Banquet Manager. I was quite keen to explore this option as I was finding work quite tiresome, due I believe to a sense of boredom emanating from the low occupancy. In any case, Sydney sounded like a good option consistent with our plans. So, I accepted the position not knowing anything about the Hyatt Kingsgate in Sydney.

Prior to departing Bali, we had the honour of being invited to a farewell dinner at the home of Prince Raka, the hereditary ruler of the island. Raka was the grandson of the last king of Bali, who actually was the ruler in practice. Raka had been educated in London and the US, and was a very sophisticated and personable individual. He was of similar age to us, and seemed to enjoy the stimulation he received from the expatriates at the Bali Hyatt.

The dinner party took place at what was formerly the palace of the king. It was a wonderful and quite humbling experience. Raka explained that as a young man he had no interest in his royal baggage, and saw no point in a titular role.

However, as he grew older he realised that his role was one of emotional support for his subjects, who simply craved an audience with him to offload their problems. He said his role was to listen to the stories of hardship, and to simply give encouragement to the individual villagers who came to see him. He did not have a lot of spare funds, but did from time to time donate to a farmer who had lost his chickens in a flood, or whose rice crop had been ruined in a storm. He realised that to the villagers he was a token of security and continuity of the old ways, and they appreciated his time and indulgence.

One interesting story from the evening relates to the former kings penchant for taking young brides. According to Raka, his grandfather had 100 wives. It was a great honour for a girl to be chosen by the king, despite there being numerous wives already in the harem. However, the story revolved around one particular wife, who was the lone survivor and still lived in the palace, but was somewhat demented.

Seemingly, on retiring for the night, it was regular routine for the king to call for one of his wives. The servant in charge would write down the name of the particular wife in a record book. Every wife's name appeared in the book, except the one who had survived. Her name was there, but it had been crossed out, as the servant had sent the wrong wife, and a different name written in its place. This obviously did not bother the king! But the surviving wife had never spent a night in the kings bed and, according to Raka, she often bemoaned this fact in her demented state.

Diplomatic Cogitation

We packed our bags and travelled to Jakarta where I contacted the Australian embassy, assuming naively that a visa would be formality, given that I was married to an Australian citizen. I met with an immigration official, and told him that I was being transferred by my company to a position in Sydney. When the official heard that I was going for work he took on a very officious approach, and advised me that, while I was entitled to a visa as the spouse of an Australian citizen, it would be necessary for me to complete various forms and await formal permission to travel. How long would this take, I enquired. At least three weeks, I was told. I explained that we were leaving Indonesia the following day, and that our exit visas had been issued by the authorities. We could not stay beyond the following day. The official said and I quote, 'let me cogitate on your situation over lunch'.

So we went off and waited while this fine representative of Australia 'cogitated' on our dilemma. When he returned, he advised us that he could not help us and that we would have to process the visa through the official channels. In other words, at least a three week wait for a visa which I was entitled to in the first place. Obviously, we were disappointed, but also somewhat stumped. We could not travel to Australia, nor could we stay in Indonesia.

We decided to head for Singapore and try our luck with the embassy there. This time I was not so transparent and applied for a tourist visa, which was issued immediately. The following day we boarded a flight bound for Perth. This was the year 1975 and the beginning of a long and happy life in the land down under.

Australia

My introduction to the country was rather eventful. We arrived at Perth airport and proceeded through customs and immigration. There were no problems with immigration, but when we got to customs we were asked to open our suitcases. Unfortunately, we could not get one of the suitcases to open. Try as we may, and with advice from a very patient customs officer, we still could not open the damn thing. Other officers gathered round with various suggestions. Then the penny dropped. The suitcase would only open if it was the right way up. We turned it over and hey presto, it opened.

After a couple of days in Perth we flew to a place called Tom Price in the remote north west of Western Australia. We went there because my wife's mother was based there in the company of her partner, who worked at the iron ore mine. Mount Tom Price is essentially a mountain of iron ore. It was discovered in 1962 with proven iron ore content of 67%, one of the highest in the world. It is, however, located in a rather inhospitable area, with a very hot climate.

The severity of the heat was brought home to me when we got a flat tyre on the way from the airport. We stopped to replace the tyre and I felt that I was going to expire with the force of the heat. Even though we had been in Bali for two years, the sheer concentration of heat was almost painful. Fortunately, my mother in law's house was airconditioned and I was welcomed with a very cold beer.

We spent a few days in that remote but quite spectacular place. The landscape is bare but quite beautiful. And the water holes in the gorges are crystal clear lagoons, offering a very cool respite from the heat.

It was then time to head to Sydney. My wife thought that a good introduction to Australia for me would be a trip by train across the Nullarbor Plain. This is a journey of some 3000 kilometres, taking two nights and three days to complete.

Nullarbor in Latin means 'no trees'. And that describes the great expanse of this flat, treeless, and arid landscape stretching forever. So, I had three days looking out the window at virtually the same view repeated for miles and miles. Might I say that this has to be the most boring trip on earth. There were nice people on the train, and even a chap who played the guitar, but for three days, I think not!

We eventually arrived in Adelaide and made our way to the Barossa Valley, a beautiful wine producing area just north of the city. My faith in Australia was restored. The Barossa valley produces some great wine, and is dotted with lots of good restaurants and cultural pursuits. It is a lovely place to spend some time.

Hyatt Kingsgate Sydney

Little did I realise it, but I had been somewhat misinformed by my colleagues in Bali, who recommended that I take on the position in Sydney. The Hyatt Kingsgate was located in Kings Cross, known as the red light district, featuring illegal casinos, brothels, and other shady enterprises. The hotel was in continual financial stress, as business levels in the city were generally difficult at that time. The hotels location was a disadvantage, being somewhat removed from the business district.

It was also a difficult hotel to operate, as it had significant physical drawbacks. Three separate towers had been connected rather inefficiently, making daily operations a continuous challenge for staff, and resulting in significant extra payroll expense. Customers were also frustrated, as the different towers and levels caused confusion.

The hospitality industry in Sydney those days was quite limited, with only three or four major hotels in the city. Indeed, hospitality was not really considered a career opportunity, apart from the availability of part time work as waiters or cleaners. Management roles were very limited given the sparsity of major hotels. The restaurant scene was also quite basic with somewhat dated food offerings.

Over the years, however, the industry evolved and Sydney now features lots of quality hotels and some really outstanding restaurants. What a turnaround! Sydney is, of course, a stunning city with a spectacular harbour bejewelled by the Opera House and the Harbour Bridge. It is now a very cosmopolitan city and international destination.

My role as Banquet Manager was extremely challenging, given the hotels layout and dire financial situation. In order to survive, the general manager, Brian Deeson, insisted on extreme cost control throughout the organisation. Payroll, being the largest expense, was severely controlled, resulting in managers literally working as an extra pair of hands.

In my case, this involved the physical set up of all meetings, conferences and banquet functions. Carrying and setting tables, vacuuming floors, handling beverage stock, arranging bars, and supervising the few casual staff who were recruited to actually serve the meals. I was in shock, and I must admit that it took me quite a while to adjust to my new surroundings.

In fact, I was so demotivated by my prospects that I actually went to the Canadian embassy seeking to return to Canada. I received permission to do so, and to this day have the stamp in my passport, 'returning emigrant'. However, my beautiful wife announced that she was pregnant with our first child, so my thoughts on returning to Canada were shelved.

I persevered and began to make some headway, with an increase in business resulting in an opportunity to hire additional staff. I was also gaining the respect of the general manager, who promoted me to assistant food and beverage manager, but still running the banquet department.

Some of my colleagues used to joke that if you asked Deeson for a raise in salary, he would give you lots of praise and encouragement, a bigger title, but no money! However, I did manage to increase my wages from $7000 per year to the lofty level of $9000. Most of my colleagues were on similar paltry wages which, given the hours we worked, was slave labour!

Cathie, a qualified nurse, secured a job in St Luke's hospital also located in Kings Cross. With both of us working at 'the cross' it was logical to seek accommodation in the area. We leased a flat in a renovated building in Ward Avenue. Little did we know that the building also housed a number of working girls, who initially used to accost me when I would be coming home very late in the evening after a banquet function.

After some time, the girls came to realise that I too was a creature of the night, and we greeted each other as fellow strugglers. I used to enquire as to business levels to which they would reply, 'lots of time for you, darling'! After a few months, we relocated to Watsons Bay, being a more appropriate location for the arrival of our first born.

Sean Michael Holland was born on August 16 1976 at the King George hospital in Sydney. I was present for the birth, which was an extraordinary experience. I was also present at the births of our daughters Sarah and Emma, also born at the King George hospital.

The Coffee Incident

Whether due to my stewardship or not, the hotel began to receive bookings for functions from the more refined end of town. The Black and White charity of upper crust society ladies held events at the hotel, as did social organisations like the Pittwater Wine and Food Society. These types of organisations were a challenge as they tended to be quite demanding, but we generally managed to satisfy them.

I recall, however, a rather difficult occasion with the Pittwater Wine and Food Society, which held their annual gala dinner at the hotel. Prior to the function, the wine and food masters of the society met with me to review every point of service in detail. The menu, aperitifs, wines, order of service, and right down to the coffee and petit fours.

The food master impressed on me the importance of the coffee, which he had provided. This he said, is a surprise. It is a very special Colombian selection not readily available in Australia. So, he impressed upon me the process necessary to ensure a proper result, even examining and testing our coffee machines. I assured him that I had the matter under control.

The evening was quite a glittering affair and went off without a hitch until the coffee! I had dispatched one of the waiters to handle the percolation of the coffee, which was to take place in the main kitchen. This waiter's name was Bruce, and, I must admit, he was not the brightest staff member. However, all I required him to do was to push a button on the coffee machine when he received word from me.

At the appointed time after the main course I called Bruce and instructed him to proceed and to call me when the coffee was ready. Not receiving a call, I went to the kitchen to find Bruce almost in tears, and telling me that the coffee was cold. He had pushed the wrong button!

I immediately went back to the function kitchen and instructed the staff to conjure up a mixture of instant coffees. Maxwell House, Nescafe, and whatever we could find were all mixed together, stirred up, and served to the unsuspecting connoisseurs. I was, of course, suffering some trepidation, until the food master rose for his after dinner speech. He went through the menu in detail, talking about each course and the origin of the food items involved.

Then he smiled and referred to the coffee. Some of you may have picked it, he said, but this is a special treat. All the way from Colombia for this special occasion, this coffee has been one of the highlights of the evening. The serving staff, who were standing to attention around the room, started to slink away fearing they were going to burst out laughing, which they did in the kitchen.

Weird Room Service

There was a rather interesting character working as a room service breakfast waiter. His name was Ken. He was gay, transvestite, and a rather large Tongan gentleman. Ken spent evenings in various joints in Kings Cross dressed in elaborate costumes and wearing lipstick, rouge and eye shadow.

Unfortunately, he would from time to time arrive for the breakfast shift straight from some nightclub, not having removed his makeup. So here he was in a hotel uniform with his fuzzy hair, large ruby red lips, layers of rouge, and with mascara dripping off his eye lashes. What a sight! And he would deliver breakfast to the unsuspecting hotel guests in this state. Well, what a shock it must have been. I recall over hearing a hotel customer relating his experience to a colleague. He said ' I opened the door to this apparition who swanned into my room with my breakfast. I thought I was hallucinating'.

Shock in the Elevator

The elevators at the Kingsgate were quite compact. Just enough room for five or six passengers. They were not designed to carry anything except the passengers, and the small trolleys used by porters and room service. Unfortunately, on one awful occasion there happened to occur a death in one of the hotel bedrooms. The ambulance was called to remove the body. In their wisdom, the ambulance attendants decided to strap the body to a stretcher and stand it up in the elevator. They also asked to have the elevator set on manual operation so that they could go straight to the ground without stopping at the various floors.

The elevator was somewhat unreliable, however, and as they descended it stopped on a particular floor where an elderly couple insisted on getting in. The ambulance attendants were nervous, but obviously did not indicate to the elderly couple what was on the stretcher. Unfortunately, in a Basil Fawlty moment, a hand appeared out the side of the stretcher. The lady customer screamed all the way to the ground floor, and had to be treated for shock by the unfortunate ambulance attendants.

Corruption at The Cross

Sydney's Kings Cross, where the hotel was located, had quite a reputation those days as the hub of all things naughty. Massage parlours, illegal bars, call girls and illegal casinos were a feature of the area. Despite very obvious evidence to the contrary, the government simply kept denying the existence of practically all of this illegal activity. However, I have personal experience of the level of corruption.

One incident relates to the annual Christmas party which the hotel used to provide for the local police, and fire departments. On one particular occasion I was chatting to the fire brigade chief, together with a senior sergeant of the police. Both had consumed a lot of alcohol and were quite inebriated. The party was held in a rather dilapidated nightclub, which the hotel did not have the funds to renovate. My inebriated guests questioned the condition of the facility and asked why the hotel did not renovate it. I advised them that it was due to of a lack of funds, to which they replied that with a little help from the fire department and the police, the place could go up in smoke and nobody would have a clue. Then we could collect the insurance and do the renovation. Simple!

On another occasion, two of the local detectives invited me to join them on a tour of The Cross after dark. This opened my eyes! We visited, and were welcomed in a number of illegal bars, and a fully functioning casino. But worse was to come. Somewhere off McCleay St., we visited the sleaziest nightclub I've ever experienced. There was pole dancing, and an array of naked Asian women performing the most amazing calisthenics with their bodies. And the place was packed with leering men, merrily drinking and cavorting. After these experiences, I was astonished to hear government ministers continue their denials. I am, however, pleased to report that most of this illegal activity was cleaned up in future years, by honest politicians and police.

Promotion

My time in banquets came to an end when the general manager promoted me to the position of Director of Rooms. He was aware of my background in the rooms department, and on the departure of my good friend, George Benney, I took on the role. I was now in charge of reception, reservations, telephones, concierge and housekeeping. I was back in my comfort zone, although I did enjoy food and beverage, but the hours were unreasonable.

Business levels were improving at the hotel, which again allowed a decent level of staffing. Service, rather than blind cost control became the priority. This approach paid dividends, with an increasing incidence of return customers.

Rock 'n Roll

One customer who caused some mirth was the illustrious Joe Cocker, of rock and roll fame. Joe checked in one evening in the company of a lady friend. He refused the assistance of a porter and made his way to his room. A little later he returned to the desk with his lady, somewhat disgruntled. 'What's going on here' he said. 'Me and my bird get to the room feeling a bit horny. We get our gear off and go to it on the bed. I'm giving her heaps, wasn't I love', he says to the lady. 'You sure were, Joe', says the lady. 'Out of the bathroom comes this Japanese bloke', he says. 'We were very embarrassed'.

The reception manager apologised profusely and upgraded Joe to a suite to compensate for the embarrassment. Obviously, the room had been double booked. The strange thing was that we never heard a word from the Japanese customer. Perhaps since the hotel was located in the red light district he was not surprised.

Career Disaster in Ireland

I was further promoted to the position of Executive Assistant Manager, which is essentially the number two in the organisation. I enjoyed this role immensely, and felt that I had significantly matured in terms of applying my management expertise. However, in the back of my mind was always the lingering curse of the emigrant, thoughts of the old country!

I had a large family of four brothers, two sisters and my mother. I also missed Ireland and, like most emigrants, only remembered the positive aspects of life there. Long summer days, green fields, jolly people and so on. No thoughts of the long cold and wet winters, or the paltry wages paid to hotel employees there at that time.

Coincident with my wistful thinking we took a holiday trip to Ireland. During the trip I noticed an advertisement for a job as the manager of a hotel, with plans for a complete redevelopment, and potential for the successful candidate to become a director of an enlarged organisation. This sounded very interesting, although there was no location or hotel name mentioned in the advertisement.

Regardless, I decided to apply and was contacted almost immediately by a certain Joe Jackson, owner of a very well established, but quite basic hotel in Ballybofey in Donegal, north west Ireland. Quite a remote location but a very scenic area. Much to the concern of my dear wife, Cathie, I attended the interview and was offered the job. It paid a reasonable salary and Jackson outlined his plans to renovate and extend the hotel.

I was aware that Jackson's son had attended the same hotel school as myself, and I enquired as to the son and heir's involvement. I was advised that the son, Barry, had plans to relocate to the US and was not interested in the project. This surprised me but I took it at face value. Little did I know that father and son were at loggerheads, and that the father had decided to bypass the son and appoint a manager. Obviously, this family feud situation was not healthy, and certainly not one with which any outsider should be involved. But I was innocent and somewhat naïve, I must admit. I decided to accept the position. What a disastrous decision!

We returned to Australia, gave notice of termination, packed our bags, and with two very young children, headed off to Ballybofey and to the worst winter in Ireland since records began! Finding a suitable house with central heating was critical, but those days most houses in Ireland were heated by boilers attached to coal fires. If the fire was not lit, the heating did not work! And my Australian wife had no experience of lighting and tending coal fires. As the winter progressed this situation became quite chronic, with Cathie struggling daily to keep the fire alight to secure heat and hot water.

My job at Jacksons hotel was a disaster. There were no plans to renovate and redevelop the property. My role was to be another pair of hands and so called manager, trying to manage a crew which included the son, daughter, and sister in law of the owner. They had their way of doing things and this was not about to change. The hotel was dirty, including the kitchens, and the rooms were in dire need of renovation. The clientele was made up of commercial travellers, wedding groups and a significant restaurant trade as the hotel featured one of the few eating venues in Ballybofey. The food was very basic but suited the clientele.

I worked endless hours, and made a feeble effort at improving the operation. Most of my initiatives were met with intransigence, as most of the staff were long term employees and saw no reason to change their ways. In addition, the owners son was essentially the manager, and had no intention of forsaking his inheritance, despite his father's advice to me that his son had plans to emigrate.

In fact, the son accosted me one evening and simply told me that I was not needed, and that he had every intention of staying and running the business. How had I been so stupid to get myself into that situation? I had made an irrational emotional decision which proved to be a near disaster for myself and my loving family. The horrible situation I had created for them was demonstrated clearly to me one cold winters afternoon when I decided to drop by our house. I found Cathie wrapped up in bed reading stories to our two children. She simply had had enough of trying to light a fire with wet coal and newspapers, and gave up. I did not blame her.

That was it. Somehow I had to rescue the situation. The first step was to quit my position at Jacksons after only five months in the job. I had stern words with the father, and advised him in no uncertain terms that I had had enough, and I walked out. When I got back to our house and told Cathie I had quit she was delighted, despite the fact that we had little money, and I was now unemployed. In fact, Jackson had not paid me the agreed salary despite my ongoing queries, and I had to resort to enlisting the help of a lawyer to secure payment.

Having no job and little money I was very fortunate that my wonderful brother Sean, and his lovely wife Kathleen, offered to have us share their home in Navan, until I found employment. This was a wonderful gesture never forgotten.

I embarked on a search for employment but Ireland was in the grip of an economic depression at that time, and jobs were very scarce. In the end, I was fortunate to find a position at the Ardboyne Hotel in Navan, and we rented a house quite close to the hotel. I vividly recall that on the day we left my brother's house our only assets were 50 pounds in the bank, and a pretty dodgy old car.

Lucky Escape

The Ardboyne was a typical country town hotel with 30 basic bedrooms, the ubiquitous busy bar, a couple of restaurants, and banquet rooms. I managed the hotel for a year or so, and began to realise that I had very limited prospects. If I did not take action, my career would be stranded.

I decided to contact Hyatt hoping I could resurrect my career. I was quite prepared to go to where ever they would choose to send me. Well, there is such a thing as the luck of the Irish! It so happened that right at this time the Hyatt in Sydney had been bought by a Singaporean by the name of Ho Whye Chung.

Mr Ho had insisted that he choose the general manager, and he nominated the chief financial officer of the hotel for the position. This did not entirely suit Hyatt as the CFO was not from the Hyatt stable, and therefore may not be entirely loyal to the Hyatt agenda. However, the owner was very aggressive and demanded that the CFO be appointed. And here is where my luck came in.

Right at that time the Hyatt Vice President received my letter seeking to rejoin the company. This presented a certain solution to the dilemma in Sydney. He decided to offer me the position of Hotel Manager with the view that I might somehow protect the Hyatt position in matters regarding the management contract, should the general manager side with the owner in such matters.

(Note: perhaps I should point out that most of the international hotel companies are management companies and do not, in most cases, own the hotels which they manage. They provide the brand name and the management under a contract with the hotel owner)

I received a phone call from the Hyatt VP asking me if I would consider returning to Sydney. Well, I was so excited at the prospect, I almost cheered. Would I consider it? I practically jumped with joy at the prospect and gave him a resounding yes! I recall then going to our house with the news and Cathie looking at me saying ' this better not be a joke' ! No, it was not a joke. I terminated my position with the Ardboyne and a few weeks later we departed for Sydney.

On arrival, we were met by the hotel General Manager, David Boward, who drove us to the hotel in a brand new car. David and I had worked together previously and were in fact, friends. On reaching the hotel David told me that the car was my company vehicle. He also mentioned that since he did not wish to live in the hotel, that we would be occupying the managers apartment. We were then ensconced in this lovely apartment overlooking Sydney harbour. A new job, new car, and deluxe apartment. What a turnaround in the fortunes of the Holland family!

Perhaps there was one saving grace about my ill feted sojourn in Ireland. Prior to my resignation from Hyatt it was suggested that my first general manager appointment would be in the holy city of Mashad, in Iran. This was the time of the Shah, and western companies were making inroads to the country. Hyatt had a number of hotels under development. I obviously missed further consideration for this position, which was taken by my former Sydney friend George Benney.

George had quite a horrific experience. Just after the hotel opened, the revolution against the Shah took place and

Mashad was the epicentre. The hotel staff became belligerently anti US and wrecked the hotel, smashing furniture, and everything they could get their hands on. George was locked in his house for a number of days fearing that he might be taken hostage. Most flights had been cancelled but he received a message from a loyal staff member that certain petroleum company executives, with whom he was familiar, were planning to depart Mashad by helicopter, and there was room for George if he could get to the airport.

George stole through the devastated hotel lobby in the early morning hours, and was covertly taken to the airport by the same trusted staff member. The helicopter was fully loaded and took off for Teheran. However, due to the weight of extra passengers, the pilot touched down in the dessert and told the passengers he would have to off load them and search for a fuel refill.

They spent some anxious hours before the helicopter returned and took them to Teheran. George then made his way to the airport, which was in a chaotic state with masses of people trying to leave the country. He managed to get a seat on an Air France plane to Paris, and then onward to Hyatt regional headquarters in Hong Kong. He arrived in Hong Kong in the clothes he had worn for five days, no luggage and no personal belongings. But he was safe. I cannot image what a horrific time my family and I might have endured had I taken the position. George was single and could travel speedily. We were four including two small children. I doubt if there would have been room in the helicopter!

Tough Owners

I was thoroughly reenergised as I started work again at the Hyatt Kingsgate. The hotel was still a challenge, but business levels were generally better in Sydney as a whole, and the hotel benefitted accordingly. The owners were a couple of brothers from Singapore. Ho Whye Chung and his younger brother, Ho Whye Tong. The older brother was the boss and he could be quite unreasonable. He seemed to have difficulty sleeping and tended to partake of the hard stuff into the wee small hours. He would then be in a foul mood the next day and castigate the general manager over every little deficiency.

As the number two, I tended to escape these harangues, and devoted my time to managing the operation. However, my time was approaching! The General Manager, David, simply could not take it anymore, and quit on the spot. The owner then berated Hyatt and demanded that they send a star performer to manage his hotel. In the meantime, I was promoted to Acting General Manager. Now I was in the firing line and copped significant abuse from Ho Whye Chung during his tirades.

The Ho's had rather grandiose and frankly unreasonable ideas regarding the Hyatt Kingsgate. They sought to provide the trappings of a five star hotel to what was essentially a four star operation at best. One of their irrational and expensive gestures was to provide the hotel with a white Rolls Royce, for the purpose of chauffeuring important customers to and from the airport.

As the hotel was not the haunt of many illustrious persons, the Rolls Royce and its designated driver were somewhat underutilised. However, this void was filled from time to time by the manager's wife, who had great fun having she and her friends chauffeured to lunch in a Rolls! And my daughter, Sarah, claims that she remembers being driven to Kindergarten in a white Rolls Royce. Perhaps this was not the intended purpose the Ho's had in mind.

Nice Girls

I had a rather interesting and unanticipated duty to perform in my role as Acting General Manager. The owners requested some female company for the visit of a couple of business clients. They insisted that these escorts be screened to ensure that they were sophisticated, and socially adept. It was suggested by my superiors that I should do the screening. I made some enquiries and managed to contact an agent who handled such matters. In fact, this gentleman invited me to his penthouse in Paddington to discuss the matter, and to impress on me that he ran a quality operation.

I found this to be fascinating and duly went to his apartment, which was quite lavish. He assured me that his ladies were all attractive and sophisticated and that a number were, in fact, visiting airline stewardesses. Others, he claimed, were single girls from good backgrounds who unashamedly sought to increase their net worth through escort activity. He also impressed upon me that he only dealt with quality clients, which is why he sought to meet me.

Well, we made arrangements and it was agreed that I would meet the two ladies in the bar of the hotel on the agreed date. I found this to be amazing. Hoteliers are all things to all people but interviewing escorts was not a role I had expected. In any case, on the evening in question, I met two very lovely outgoing and amiable ladies, and we chatted over a drink about the project ahead. I then gave them the directions to the hotel suite and said goodnight. I heard no more but was very keen to find out how the evening worked out. It was not until some weeks later that I had a call from headquarters noting that the owners were very impressed with the provided entertainment. The things we innkeepers do!

Lost Dinner

As I have said, the layout of the hotel presented many operating challenges. This was proven when my wife and I ordered our dinner through room service. The mangers apartment was located on top of one of the three towers. In order to gain access one had to take the elevator to the top floor, and then walk up a further flight of steps. Not the easiest place to find if unfamiliar with the layout.

On this occasion there was a new waiter on duty and he was despatched with the dinner order. After a very long time I enquired of the room service order taker as to the whereabouts of our dinner. The order taker expressed surprise that I had not received it, indicating that the waiter had left over half an hour ago. Eventually, a rather embarrassed young waiter arrived at our apartment. He had been up and down the various towers in three different elevators searching for the managers apartment. He even ended up in the shopping plaza attached to the hotel. Obviously, the food was pretty spoiled by the time he reached our apartment, but we were amused by the story and the thought of this young chap meandering through the complex with our dinner on a tray.

On Strike

During this time, the hotel union decided to go on strike. They initially called for rolling two day strikes each week. That way the staff still received their wages but for two days the hotel had very few workers. Under union employer agreements, only management and apprentices were allowed to work in a formal strike situation. This makes life difficult in a 400 bedroom hotel. And the strike took place in October, the busiest time of the year. I should also note that the licencee's spouse is also entitled to work, with my wife Cathie being called into action.

The hotels in the city decided to confront the union, as their demands were considered unreasonable. It was therefore decided that we would continue to operate but advise customers of limited service. This entailed the service of breakfast only, no other meals, no room service, and tables in the lobby with soap and towels on a help yourself basis. However, the bedrooms had to be serviced, and this was the biggest challenge. Especially when the strike developed to a complete withdrawal of labour.

The management team of GM, CFO, Personnel, Purchasing, Rooms and secretarial staff formed teams and took on the job of cleaning bedrooms each morning. This was initially fun but wore thin after some time. Having cleaned the bedrooms, we would then proceed to the banquet area in the evening to assist with meal service. My wife featured greatly as a banquet waitress. On one occasion a customer asked her what her normal role was, to which Cathie replied, 'I'm normally the managers wife'. The customer was very impressed at such commitment and support for her man!

The cleaning of the rooms was hard work, especially as the hotel was fully booked and the workload was quite confronting. But we had some fun. We allocated the tasks with someone cleaning bathrooms, others making beds and others vacuuming. The personnel manager decided that the most efficient way to clean the bathrooms was to fill a bucket with water and splash it onto the floors. He would then return with a mop and mop the floors. Unfortunately, thinking a particular room was vacant, he opened the bathroom door and splashed the water around, much to the consternation of a customer sitting on the toilet. Wrong room!

Each evening we would have a few beers and many laughs. There was a great sense of camaraderie among the team, but as the strike continued into its third week, I could sense a level of tiredness and frustration developing. I started to worry as to our prospects of holding out. Just then a trickle of staff members started drifting back to work, despite the unions cajoling. The trickle quickly became a flood and the strike was over.

I wondered how many more days we would have lasted, but I was delighted that the staff proved more loyal to the hotel and their jobs than to the union. I certainly respect the place of unions and the need for them in protecting workers from unscrupulous employers, and there are some employers who would simply take advantage, if they could. So, I am not a union basher, never have been.

I was in the role of Acting GM for the best part of a year and I was confident that the hotel operation was trending in the right direction. Hyatt was still searching to identify the star GM to take over the role. At this time I was visited by a Hyatt Vice President, who congratulated me on my performance in managing the hotel, but said that they could not tell the owner that the star he was looking for was there already.

So, it was made clear to me that if I wanted my own hotel I would have to relocate when they found the star. A short time later a chap called Jon Richards was appointed and I was drafted to the Hyatt Bumi Surabaya, in Indonesia.

Surabaya Indonesia.

Surabaya is the second city of Indonesia. It is located in East Java quite close to the Bali strait, which separates Java from Bali. The official population was two million, but was unofficially closer to three. Those days Indonesia was ruled by a military dictatorship under President Soharto. The military had divided up the country with the army ruling Jakarta, and the navy in charge of Surabaya and its environs. The Indonesian fleet was based in Surabaya, as was the admiral of the fleet, Rudolf Kasenda.

As a result, all sorts of supply companies sent their representatives to the city seeking to do business with the navy. These business deals included armaments, engines, logistics, patrol boats, and every item required to operate and maintain a navy. In addition, East Java was and still is, the centre of the tobacco growing industry, with manufacturing plants producing clove cigarettes, so beloved by Indonesian smokers. As such, tobacco traders and consultants were frequent visitors to the area. So with the activity generated by the navy and the tobacco industry, Surabaya was a thriving commercial centre. It was, however, quite a dirty poorly maintained metropolis, with inadequate drainage and sanitation, and prone to major flooding in the rainy season.

The city was also short of quality hotel accommodation with one significant exception, the Hyatt Bumi. The hotel was a stunningly white building in the midst of an otherwise drab environment. It featured 250 quality rooms with fine restaurants, function facilities, swimming pool and a pub. It was a beacon of sophistication in a rather underdeveloped and overcrowded city. As a result, almost every international business executive, and Indonesian government representative, sought accommodation at the Hyatt. It was the only decent game in town! And being the manager of this oasis certainly ensured a high profile for the individual concerned.

The hotel was owned by a Jakarta based insurance company who had an owners representative stationed at the hotel. This tends to be the modus operandi of hotel owning companies. The company enters into a contract with a hotel management company and then appoints a company representative to manage the contract, and to ensure compliance on the part of the hotel management company. Unfortunately, this arrangement can be somewhat fraught, should the owners representative misinterpret the role and consider that they have greater authority than the management company general manager. Or simply if the owners representative embarks on a mission to prove his or her worth, by interfering in the operation of the hotel. This is an all too common occurrence and leads to endless friction.

On the other hand, it should be noted that there are many examples of level headed owners representatives, who understand that their role should be one of support. In these instances both parties contribute greatly to the success of the hotel, with customers, staff, and owning and management companies reaping the benefits.

Unfortunately, in Surabaya at the time of my arrival, the owning company representative was a rather unstable and deceitful individual. He took an instant dislike to me, for no rational reason. He continually called me to his office to discuss what can only be referred to as inconsequential and nebulous issues. These issues mostly related to the level of respect he demanded from the hotel management.

However, over and above regular reporting and general respectful interaction with this individual, it was impossible to know what really irked him. But he was not a happy camper, and continually made negative comments about the management i.e. me. I could only put it down to chemistry. He simply did not like me! This individual sought to poison the mind of the owning company towards me, and also to negatively influence my boss, that Andre Pury again, who was based in Singapore. A rather unpleasant atmosphere ensued for quite a while, making life difficult.

However, some months into my term in Surabaya the chairman of the owning company came to stay in the hotel. He called me to his suite one Sunday morning and was almost obsequious in his apologies to me. 'Our company representative has been very unfair to you, Mr Holland' he said. 'He spread lies about your performance in an effort to distract our company from his own wrongful deeds. We have audited his office and found a significant case of embezzlement. He has been dismissed, and we are taking legal action against him. On behalf of our company, I must apologise to you profusely'. I was astonished but there was more good news. The chairman appointed a new owners representative with specific instructions not to interfere in the hotel operation, and more to the point, to ensure that Mr Holland gets the utmost support from the owning company. My work life from then onwards was a dream!

The term 'Bapak' means father in the Indonesian language. Often the head of a company or business will be referred to as Bapak by the employees. The term relates to the responsibilities of the boss not only to be the leader and decision maker, but also to be the benefactor and carer for the staff of the enterprise. It carries great respect and trust. Some six months into my time in Surabaya my secretary came to give me good news. 'Today, she said, I heard you being referred to as Bapak for the first time. You have been accepted by the staff, Mr Holland' This was a great honour!

Indonesia was still a very corrupt society those days. However, I never once had an occasion where I had to offer or authorise bribes to any government official. Of course, I certainly was approached by local officials seeking special treatment for their visiting superiors from Jakarta. On these occasions I would simply afford them a discounted room rate, and ensure that the boss from Jakarta was upgraded to superior accommodation. This endeared the local official to myself and the hotel, and ensured cooperation in any subsequent dealings with officialdom.

An example of this cooperation was an occasion when my wife was travelling to Sydney to give birth to our second daughter, Emma. I had forgotten to secure Cathie's exit visa, a document necessary for anyone wishing to depart the country. I only realised my oversight when my secretary alerted me to it the day before Cathie's departure. With much embarrassment and apologies we contacted the head of Immigration who actually sent an officer to our apartment to issue the visa. There was no waiting in hot smelly offices, and the visa was issued immediately. This was indicative of the spirit of cooperation to which I refer.

Some months later Cathie was chatting to the wives of some of our expatriate friends when the subject of exit visas was raised. The other ladies were complaining about having to complete a myriad of forms, and spend hours in the immigration office in order to attain a visa. 'Don't they come to your house to issue the visa' Cathie naively enquired! This was met with some astonishment on the part of the beleaguered ladies.

The frequent use of the hotel by visiting government officials was good for business and, on one specific occasion very helpful, in an inverse way, to solving a major problem. This relates to an incident where the main electricity cable supplying the hotel which ran under the carpark, was damaged, and the hotel power supply failed.

The local electricity company sent along a bunch of workers to dig up the carpark and locate and repair the cable. This was the rainy season with torrents of tropical rain on a daily basis. The workers dug a huge pit in the carpark and located the cable. However, the pit filled with water very quickly despite their best efforts to keep the area dry. They made fruitless attempts to reconnect the cable, but each time it became sodden with rain water and just about exploded when they threw the switch to restore power. This was very dangerous and simply irresponsible on the part of the electricity company.

In the meantime, the hotel was getting warmer by the day. Customers were departing in search of accommodation with air conditioning and lighting. There was no solution in sight, as the maintenance crew working on fixing the problem seemed incapable of resolving the issue. It was then that I became aware that a senior minister of the government was booked into the hotel and due to arrive the next day.

In such instances, the governor of the area is required to act as host to a visiting minister, to ensure the visitor's comfort and security. I contacted the governor's office and told them that the hotel had no electricity and, as a consequence, no air conditioning. Hardly a welcoming prospect for a senior minister. In such circumstances the governor would have no option but to invite the minister to stay at the governor's own residence.

In this particular case, the governor had a fervent and personal dislike of the minister. There was no way he wanted this minister staying at his home. The governor enquired as to the cause of the power interruption, and was advised that the matter had been in train for a number of days and the electricity company could not resolve the problem. The governor then contacted the navy and instructed them to apply all their expertise to fix the problem. Almost immediately a troop of navy engineers arrived at the hotel. They drilled a large hole in the wall of the hotel, connected power cables from the main street into the hotel transformer and, within hours, the power was restored. It was pretty impressive. The minister checked in the next day none the wiser of the governor's intervention.

A Funny Funeral.

The pub at the Bumi Hyatt was a place of refuge for the expatriate community living in the city. Often these souls had to endure power failures affecting their home comforts. No power meant no water, no refrigeration, and no air conditioning, making life quite unbearable. On such occasions, which were quite frequent, the pub would be thronged with expatriates escaping the rigours of suburban life in Surabaya. Indeed, many of these people took rooms in the hotel and stayed until power was restored.

One regular of the pub was a retired English tobacco merchant, named Mike Sumner. Mike had retired in Surabaya despite the fact that he no longer had a visa to stay in the country. His visa had been attached to his work position and was cancelled when he retired. As a result, Mike was somewhat a prisoner as he could not leave the country for fear of being refused re-entry. He simply decided to stay put and actually never left. I suppose this is understandable as Mike was not close to his family who resided in the UK, and, having spent twenty five years in Surabaya, he had no other home.

He was a hail fellow well met, as they say. Big and loud and forever in a jovial mood. He simply dominated the company in the pub night after night. However, Mike died rather suddenly from a heart attack. This was a shock to all who knew him and his funeral was attended by a great cross section of locals and expatriates.

Mike would have roared with laughter, however, had he witnessed the chaotic scenes at the funeral. It happened to be the monsoon season and on driving through the cemetery to the crematorium, the hearse became bogged in a pool of mud. The driver revved the vehicle resulting in the back door opening and the coffin falling out into the mud. The wreaths of flowers also toppled out. A few strong men managed to lift the coffin back into the hearse and to push the hearse out of the quagmire.

Then at the crematorium, Mike's son who had travelled from the UK, was asked to light the fire. A rather macabre thing, I thought. Unfortunately, the fire would not light and the coffin simply disappeared into a recess. It was then returned and the unfortunate son tried again to no avail. He broke down and mumbled all sorts of insults about this stupid place! Mike would have laughed.

On the way out of the cemetery, I noticed that a bunch of local children had made posies from the flowers in the wreaths, which they'd saved from the mud and were offering them for sale to the funeral congregation. Very entrepreneurial, I thought.

Gudang Garam

Gudang Garam is the second largest clove cigarette manufacturer in Indonesia, and one of the largest employers. During my time in Surabaya the company was owned by a Chinese Indonesian business man, Rachman Halim, who was one of the richest people in the country. The business was based in Kediri, about 100 kilometres from Surabaya. The company looked after its employees providing medical facilities, schools and regular income. Its managers and supervisors were provided with accommodation in company built housing. In general, the owner was a benefactor, and highly regarded by the people of Kediri.

The pending marriage of the son and heir presented the owner with a challenge in how to provide the best possible food and service for the wedding guests. Facilities in Kediri were basic at best and could not possibly handle the occasion. He decided that the only solution was to enlist the help of the Hyatt in Surabaya. We were approached and somewhat taken aback when told of the task's magnitude. There were to be 5000 guests for the wedding luncheon, followed by

1200 very special invitees for dinner in the evening. And the site was 100 kilometres from the hotel. The question was if we could handle it.

I suppose money overcomes most problems, and in the case of Gudang Garam, there was no scarcity of funds. Some significant logistical planning was embarked upon by our head chef and food and beverage manager. Apart from the preparation of so much food, there was the challenge of getting it to Kediri in a wholesome state. Mr Halim came to the rescue, advising us that his company would provide refrigerated trucks. In addition, since a number of his esteemed guests would be driving to the venue, he provided funds to the local council to resurface the main road all the way from Surabaya to Kediri.

He also contacted his favourite cake shop in Surabaya and asked the owner to provide an enormous order of cakes for the wedding. The owner was embarrassed to advise him that she did not have the capacity in her small bakery to cope with the large order. Halim arranged to have the bakery extended at his expense so that the order could be filled. The bakery owner not only received a significant payment for the cakes but ended up with a larger and totally refurbished bakery.

On the occasion of the wedding, the factory managers were asked to vacate their company houses so that the VIPs could be accommodated. Cathie and I were lucky enough to be considered VIPs, and had the comfort of the very adequate staff housing. The wedding was a very impressive affair and, to my relief, the food and service was most satisfactory.

The owner instructed Hyatt to focus entirely on the food operation and to leave the drink service to his company. Being unfamiliar with beverage handling, they simply placed a bottle of Dom Perignon champagne and a bottle of Hennessy XO brandy on every table. The champagne was at room temperature, which is pretty hot in Indonesia. This was unfortunate, but the Hyatt food and beverage manager managed to provide an ice bucket for the champagne on the Holland table! VIPs indeed!

Golf has played a significant part in my life and travels. I tend to be a golf fanatic, despite never really mastering the game. In Surabaya, I joined the Yani Golf Club and spent many enjoyable hours there. This was good public relations, as most of the Indonesian government hierarchy played golf and were members of the club.

One of the most popular annual tournaments was the Bumi Hyatt Cup. With the hotel providing quality food and beverage as well as abundant prizes, every member of the club sought to be involved. In this way, I developed friendships with many of the local officials, including a navy general who was responsible for civic order in the city. His name was Gatot Sularto, who was a very personable and socially adept individual. However, he was a very powerful and feared individual when it came to the issue of public order.

On one occasion, a group of gang members created some mayhem in the hotel night club. This was a serious incident where a knife was drawn, and threats made to staff and other patrons. The hotel security managed to calm the situation, but not without some serious concern for their safety. Shortly thereafter, I was contacted by Sularto enquiring about the incident. I had not reported it, so this was evidence of how informed he was. He advised me to call him immediately should any further incidents occur.

A few weeks later the same gang members again started a ruckus in the night club. I contacted Sularto and within minutes an armoured car arrived at the hotel and a troop of navy commandoes entered the night club and removed the gang members. They took them to the carpark and gave them a drubbing. Order was restored, and never again did we experience any similar trouble.

While in Surabaya, I decided to apply for Australian citizenship. In my mind, Australia had become my home base, and I felt that I should identify with the country. I was invited to the Australian Embassy in Jakarta to formalise the matter but there was one element of the ceremony which somewhat bothered me.

At that time, it was necessary to swear allegiance to the Queen in order to secure citizenship. For an Irish republican, this aspect of the process presented some conscientious objection. But there was no consideration for such objection at that time. In more recent times, candidates for citizenship have the option of swearing an oath of allegiance to the country, using the bible or other books of faith. So, I had a dilemma! My conscience was eased, however, when a friend told me that if one crosses ones fingers while swearing allegiance, then it does not count. This is a rather doubtful superstitious type of principle but I suppose such things are a matter of inner belief. My citizenship ceremony was conducted in the office of a consular official. When we came to swear the oath, I put my hands in my pockets and crossed my fingers. The official smiled and said,' I know what you are doing but it doesn't bother me'. So, I avoided swearing allegiance to the crown of England. Or did I?

New Hyatt Boss

I spent three years in Surabaya. The posting was normally for two years, but at that time a certain Bernd Chorengal was appointed President of Hyatt International.

Chorengal was a rather aggressive individual. He was, however, very clear in his objectives for the Hyatt organisation internationally. He let it be known that he intended to terminate the contracts on hotels which he felt were not up to the required standard. In addition, and somewhat worrying for everybody, he announced that certain general managers would also be terminated, as they too weren't performing to a high enough standard.

This sent certain shock waves throughout the company and, with the reduction in the number of hotels, there were few opportunities for managers to transfer. Everyone stayed where they were, assuming they were not going to be removed. So, instead of two years, I spent an additional year in Surabaya. I must say that my third year was the most enjoyable. When the Indonesians take you to their heart, and you no longer intimidate them, they become friends for life. They are a warm, family orientated people, with great charm, and are almost always smiling. This is what I experienced in my third year and it was delightful.

Chorengal was a go getter and achieved many great things for Hyatt International. He took a company which was struggling to gain traction and turned it into a very significant and successful international corporation through the sheer force of his personality. He took no prisoners. He was very successful and was responsible for enlarging and energising the Hyatt brand around the world. However, a few decent individuals fell by the wayside in the process.

Kuala Lumpur.

The Prime Minister of Malaysia, Mahatir Bin Mohamad, had great aspirations to modernise his otherwise sleepy society. He ruled Malaysia with an iron fist, brooking little or no opposition. One of his many initiatives was to develop a golf resort in Kuala Lumpur similar to a project he experienced in Tokyo. It had two 18 hole championship golf courses, and an international hotel. Mahatir felt that Kuala Lumpur was ready for such a facility, as apart from the prestigious and very private Royal Selangor Golf Club, the city at that time was bereft of quality golfing.

He therefore instructed his team to embark on identifying a site suitable for the development of 36 holes of golf, and a major hotel facility. Thus was born the Hyatt Saujana Hotel and Country Club located at Subang, in close proximity to what was then Kuala Lumpur International Airport. This was to be my next project and, having farewelled Surabaya, my family and I arrived in Kuala Lumpur in 1985, with the hotel due to open in 1986.

The opening of a hotel can be very challenging, and lots of fun. The Hyatt Saujana was, unfortunately, extremely challenging indeed. The owning company, Peremba, was a quasi government organisation, set up by the government to plan and own commercial properties. The company executives tended to be members of the United Malay National Party or UMNO, which was the political party of the government. These executives were not particularly competent, gaining their positions through political patronage rather than ability.

When I arrived on site, the golf courses were already operating, as was a rather lavish golf club house. These facilities were initially managed by the owning company but taken over later by Hyatt management. My job was to establish the hotel operation of 250 rooms, banquet facilities and restaurants. The design was resort style with three blocks of rooms planned, each block with a central courtyard.

I set about reviewing plans, interviewing and hiring management, and addressing the host of issues involved in a hotel opening. The structural skeleton of the hotel was already in place, but there was much work to be completed.

Initial board meetings with the owning company tended to be somewhat fraught with tension. I could not exactly put my finger on the reason, but I was certainly aware of significant anxiety, especially when matters of finance were discussed such as funding for payroll, promotion, uniforms, linen, foodstuffs, and the myriad of supplies necessary to commence operations.

Board members became nervous and tended to question every item of expenditure. Discussions tended to be meandering and quite meaningless. The funding required was entirely in accordance with budgets previously presented by Hyatt and approved by the board. However, this did not quell the obvious discomfort on the part of the board members.

I did, however, manage to determine the reason for the ongoing challenges to already approved budget items. The board had considerably overspent on the development of the golf courses and the clubhouse. They realised that they did not have sufficient funds to complete the hotel construction, and certainly not for the operational requirements as previously listed. But the real issue was that none of the directors was prepared to be the bearer of such bad news to the Prime Minister.

So, after a few months of posturing, the board instructed their representative, a Malay Indian gentleman by the name of Ravi, to inform me that the hotel project would not continue and that I should leave. It was also suggested that the contract with Hyatt would be terminated. Obviously, this came as a shock not only to me but also to my boss, Andre Pury, the Hyatt Vice President.

Andre's reaction was that Hyatt was under contract to provide management services and that I should maintain my presence so that the company is seen to be carrying out its duties under the contract. Should the owning company wish to terminate the contract then this must be done through appropriate channels, and not by a verbal message at the work site.

I relayed this message to Ravi, who was not very pleased, and considered me ridiculous to maintain a presence when the hotel was not going to open. Shortly thereafter all work ceased and the contractors withdrew. My team was now in the invidious position of feeling unwelcome with their jobs in jeopardy.

The Prime Minister had also commenced a much more significant project than a golf resort. He had managed to set up the production of Malaysia's own automobile, the Proton Saga. He was particularly proud of this project and was the owner of one of the first cars off the production line. One of his great pleasures was to go for a drive on a Sunday in his new Proton Saga, much to the consternation of his security detail.

One particular Sunday in the midst of our stop work dilemma, he decided to drive to the resort to check out the progress. Both my assistant Peter Stettler and I happened to be present, and we were alerted by a very excited security guard that the Prime Minister was at the main entrance. This was an unfinished main entrance with scaffolding and construction equipment still strewn all over the place. We rushed out to meet our illustrious guest, who was somewhat perturbed at the state of the project.

'I was given to understand that the hotel was already operating' he told us. Unfortunately, we said, that is not the case, and the site has been idle for a number of weeks. The Prime Minister was visibly embarrassed and upset by this information. We thanked him for his visit and he advised us that he would have to look into the matter.

Well, one can imagine the berating some individuals must have borne after the PM's visit. To our great surprise and relief, all the contractors returned to the job the following Monday morning. One can only assume that the board members must have felt some relief that it was the Hyatt representatives who were the bearers of the bad news, and not one of them. Some six months later the hotel opened.

Coolum

The Hyatt organisation experienced significant growth in the eighties. Chorengal was aggressively seeking contracts all over the world, with significant success. There was a particular interest in Australia, where developers were keen to be involved in hotel and resort projects. During this time Hyatt became involved in projects in Melbourne, Adelaide, Canberra, Sanctuary Cove and on the Sunshine Coast, in a sleepy but beautiful area known as Coolum.

I attended a Hyatt General Managers meeting in Macau, where Chorengal proudly presented a list of the projects the company was working on worldwide. I was particularly interested in Australia, as the country had become my home base and our children would soon require educational stability. I had indicated my desire to return to Australia, should the appropriate opportunity arise.

One of the projects presented by Chorengal was known at that time as the Hyatt Coeur de Lion. This was the Coolum project. The name related to the health fundamentals involved in the project. It had been conceived by a Melbourne based doctor, John Tickell, who was very much involved in what he described as corporate health. He espoused the notion that overworked corporate executives were suffering from dangerous levels of stress, and needed to take stock. He was one of the first medicos to warn of these dangers and the attendant consequences of unmanaged stress leading to too much alcohol, poor diet and broken relationships. He touched a nerve, and became a popular presenter on television talk shows, as well as company boardrooms.

Tickell developed the idea of establishing a resort where stressed out corporate executives could spend time, and receive help dealing with their problems. He envisaged a haven of tranquillity where health specialists would assist clients in matters of stress management, diet, exercise routines, and general wellness. It was to be a place where people would 'find their true spirits again' away from the rigours of daily life. In addition, there would be lectures on life and business management, presented by experts in the field. All in all, this was a wonderful concept but somewhat ahead of its time for Australia.

Some of the fundamentals of the concept were a copy of a similar project in California known as La Costa Resort. However, La Costa was somewhat more commercial and less stringent than that proposed by Tickell for Coolum. Tickell's resort would not welcome children, would not be open to the public, and would be focused on tranquillity. All were welcome at La Costa, and its location in the mega rich California environment just about guaranteed success.

Coolum was chosen for a number of attributes. It was close to an airport, was on the beach, had a good climate, and the land was very cheap. All Tickell needed was a developer prepared to provide the funding, and a hotel company prepared to provide the management and marketing.

At that time the Japanese economy was booming, with interest rates in Japan at an all time low. Japan's government encouraged companies to invest offshore, resulting in rivers of funds becoming available for projects all over the world. Australia received its fair share, with Japanese investment in resorts, hotels, shopping malls, apartments, railways and so on.

Doctor John Tickell was a very clever character. He managed to make contact with Kumagai Gumi, a Japanese construction company which was very keen to identify opportunities in a stable country like Australia. Tickell presented his project and indicated that he had an option on the land, and that he was in discussions with the Hyatt organisation as potential managers of the resort. This greatly impressed the executives at Kumagai Gumi and they expressed significant interest.

Tickell then travelled to Chicago to meet with the Hyatt boss, Chorengal. He advised Chorengal that he had the land and that he had a major investor in Kumagai Gumi. This in turn greatly impressed Chorengal, who loved the essence of the project, and became enthralled with the entire concept. Chorengal advised Tickell to develop plans for the project and to return to Chicago when the deal was signed with Kumagai Gumi. Tickell then revisited Kumagai and informed them that Hyatt had indicated their involvement, which sealed the deal with Kumagai.

Just A Simple Innkeeper | 145

Now Tickell could develop the draft plans and return to Chorengal for approval. This he did, but when Chorengal reviewed the initial plans he disliked the traditional hotel building which was being proposed. He advised Tickell to instruct the architects to spread the accommodation units throughout the very large site. This instruction was carried out, regardless of the operational inefficiencies it would create in a country where wage control was of the essence. This decision made the resort very labour intensive in a very high wage cost environment.

At the General Managers meeting in Macau, Chorengal in his presentation referred to the Coolum project as being quite unique in the world, and requiring particular General Manager skills. I was therefore surprised when I was called to a meeting with Chorengal where he indicated that my boss in Kuala Lumpur, Andre Pury, had recommended me for the role in Coolum. He said, 'I don't really know you but I have confidence in Andre's recommendation'. I was of course somewhat flattered by this recognition. However, I did harbour some deep concerns about Coolum's whole concept. But I needed to visit the project, meet the owners and determine how to approach the role.

A few weeks later, Cathie and I travelled to Coolum to visit the site and to meet the parties involved. I was absolutely astonished at the natural beauty of the Coolum area. In addition, I was impressed with the progress on the site and the fact that the construction was ahead of schedule.

The resort was to feature 156 hotel rooms and 168 villas, with most of the villas having two bedrooms and the more lavish ones having three. In total this represented 510 bedrooms and bathrooms. This was a very significant rooms inventory to place in such a remote destination. The developers included plans to sell the villas in quarter shares to prospective investors in a scheme similar to time share.

The property covered a total of 150 hectares or approximately 350 acres of grounds, and included a championship golf course, tennis complex, a lavish spa, retail, restaurants, an art centre, and a very significant piece of rain forest. Not to mention a one kilometre beach front, and nine swimming pools dotted throughout.

The golf course was designed by the world renowned designer, Robert Trent Jones Jr. The conceptual architectural design of the resort was developed by the illustrious firm of WATG from Hawaii, and executed by the Brisbane based Bligh Voller. Collateral design was by the noted designer, Michael Bryce. All in all the pedigrees of the consultants were beyond question, and the planned resort was simply outstanding.

The spa at the resort was to be the epicentre of the health concept. Apart from offering an array of spa treatments, it was to feature dietitians, doctors, and even a medical laboratory conducting pathology tests.

What a proposition this mega resort was turning out to be! And every aspect of the operation was to be managed by Hyatt. So here I was, the itinerant hotel manager, about to become the overall leader of this multifaceted complex. How exciting!

Filled with awe and enthusiasm for my future prospects, I returned to Kuala Lumpur after my short trip to Coolum and alerted my boss that Coolum was ahead of schedule, and that I needed to be relieved of my duties at Hyatt Saujana as soon as possible. This was arranged, and I was then required to travel to Hyatt headquarters in Chicago for a briefing on the Coolum project. Little did I know what challenges lay ahead.

Chicago

Essentially, Coolum was the pet project of the Hyatt President, Bernd Chorengal. He loved the cutting edge aspect of the concept. This was not simply a resort, but a destination designed to help high flying corporate executives with better choices in both physical and mental wellbeing. In addition, there would be guidance on how to better manage a demanding enterprise and how to be good corporate citizens.

Chorengal paid little heed to the practicality of market feasibilities, and the limited scope for such a product in the comparatively small Australian market. There were already a number of much smaller health retreats operating on a much more modest but similar principle, and they were struggling for financial viability. None of these facts concerned him.

I spent a week with the various vice presidents of the company discussing the project. Without exception, vice presidents of technical support, food and beverage, marketing, finance and human resources, all indicated grave concern for the viability of the Coolum project. It was too large, it was in a remote location, it had limited conference facilities, it was operationally a nightmare with the accommodation units spread throughout the complex in such a high wage cost environment. Simply put, all of these senior Hyatt executives 'canned' the project. Obviously, this was not very encouraging for one about to take on the management of such a hybrid.

At the end of my week of familiarisation, I was invited to a debriefing with the President and his Vice Presidents. This took place in a round table discussion where the President opened by asking me what my thoughts were. I indicated my enthusiasm for the uniqueness of the project and for the natural beauty of the destination. However, I also indicated my serious concern for the fact that the resort would feature the hotel equivalent of 510 bedrooms but was not to be equipped with a major conference facility necessary to fill so many rooms.

The president was aghast at my lack of understanding of the concept. He said, ' you have been in Chicago for one week and still do not understand the concept. We do not do large conferences at Coolum, we do boutique conferences. You need to read the concept statement and follow it to the letter' and with that he left the room. I have to say that apart from the effects of this put down from the president, I was very disappointed that not one of his vice presidents was prepared to offer me support, despite all of them having expressed grave concerns during my one to one briefings. They were simply in fear of the great man!

So, I departed Chicago with strict instructions to carry out a mission which I knew to be untenable. I was very much aware that, given the size and scope of the job at hand, that I would be fully occupied preparing for the opening, but I did harbour major fears for the future. The level of business necessary to make the project financially viable was quite huge, but given the limited conference facilities, the seasonal nature of the market, and the labour intensive nature of the project, I knew we had our work cut out! And a further fundamental flaw in the concept was the fact that children were to be discouraged from staying at the resort. What a nonsense this was in a market where successful corporate executives tended to holiday with their families. Yes, total nonsense!

World Tour

One rather enjoyable aspect of my familiarisation program for Coolum was the fact that it was decided that I required exposure to some luxury spa destinations, to see how it is done, so to speak. The choice of destination was somewhat optional, but someone in Hyatt suggested Champneys in London, The Hunt Spa in Dallas, and La Costa in California on which Coolum was modelled. In addition, I visited the Hyatt resorts in Hawaii on my way home. Well, this was really hard work, I must say. Having to expose my body to all sorts of exotic treatments delivered by comely therapists was over and above the call of duty. I arrived back in Australia rejuvenated and forever a spa convert.

Pre-Opening

I set about identifying key personnel. Firstly, I needed to find a personal assistant, so I advertised the position and was deluged with applications. In the end I whittled the short list down to 15 candidates, and commenced interviews. My office was temporarily located in one of the completed villas, right in the middle of a rather messy and muddy work site. The unfortunate interviewees, all female, arrived dressed in their finery, and had to make their way through the site in high heels, accompanied by wolf whistles from the workers. By the time they reached my office they were somewhat hot and bothered with shoes plastered in mud.

Over a few of days I interviewed 14 of the 15 applicants and could not decide on who would be right for me and the job. They were each very competent in their own way and all were pleasant and presentable. The final applicant, Anne Callanan, arrived in early afternoon, but I was rather tied up with a delegation of Hyatt executives and had to keep Anne waiting for quite a long period of time. I was very apologetic when I finally commenced our interview. Almost immediately, however, I felt that she was the right person for the job. She was composed, pleasant and presented very well. She was totally unfazed by the circuitous route to my office, and the interminable wait for her interview. Whatever chemistry existed between us I will never know, but Anne Callanan became my personal assistant, and worked with me for the next 20 years. What a find!

With so many projects opening around the world, the Hyatt organisation became very short of in house talent. In fact, I was advised by the Hyatt Vice President of Human Resources that I would have to search for senior management candidates on the open market, as Hyatt simply could not provide them. Obviously this presented the challenge of not only finding the right people, but of also imparting Hyatt philosophies and orientation to senior managers. Only four members of the original management team had previous Hyatt experience. However, I was lucky enough to identify some outstanding people from within Australia.

Fundamentally, the resort was a high quality product. It consisted of clusters of rooms and villas grouped around a guest lounge where customers were to be served breakfast and evening cocktails. The whole resort was designated Regency Club, which is the Hyatt version of the Executive Floor. In addition, there was an exclusive area featuring luxury villas and residences known as the Ambassadors Club. This area featured a swimming pool, tennis courts, and a guest lounge for Ambassador customers.

The selection of tableware, linen, collateral, stationary, and every single element of service were all consistent with the high quality infrastructure. In my search for unique and appropriate uniform design, I contacted the Rae Ganim fashion design company who responded with enormous energy and enthusiasm for the whole resort concept, with Rae and her husband, Anthony, becoming the keepers of the uniform portfolio. Rae and Anthony simply lived for the project and produced unique and outstanding employee outfits. In fact, the uniforms were so impressive that President Chorengal instructed me to send samples to the various Hyatt resorts around the world, as guidance for their uniform selection.

Employment Opportunites

There was great excitement in the local Coolum and Sunshine Coast community with the pending opening of the Hyatt. Prospects for employment, as well as potential business opportunities in supplying the forthcoming operation, created significant interest. The majority of the people were extremely positive about the resort development, and saw it as the first major step in establishing the destination in the world of tourism. It also represented long term employment prospects for the children of local residents, as there was serious unemployment on the coast, particularly among the younger population.

I was approached by the local director of the Commonwealth Employment Service, who indicated to me that he had on his files a number of young adults who he thought could be trained to work in the resort. I said that we would be more than willing to help these young people, and that we would provide them with the necessary training. He thanked me for my cooperation and we agreed that he would identify 40 people whom he considered suitable. Arrangements were made for this group to commence employment and training approximately one month before the opening.

The first indication of concern, however, was the fact that five of the group simply did not turn up. This was disappointing, but we were pleased that the other 35 seemed keen to pursue the opportunity. Unfortunately, much to our disappointment, and to the embarrassment of the Director of the CES, some three months after the resort had opened, all but one of these individuals had resigned and gone back on the dole. As one local said to me at the time, ' if you are young and being paid not to work, and can spend your day surfing, why bother'. Pity.

Apart from this disappointment, we hired over 400 locals as waiters, cooks, gardeners, golf staff, receptionists, therapists, tennis staff, retail staff, and maintenance technicians. All were trained and inculcated with the Hyatt service philosophies. And all were excited to be part of such a magnificent dream.

Name Change

After much soul searching, and some less than positive market feedback, both Hyatt and the owning company agreed to change the name of the resort. The Hyatt Coeur de Lion was simply too much of a mouthful for the market, so the name was changed to The Hyatt Regency Coolum. This was more in keeping with Hyatt branding worldwide and softened to an extent the health connotation. Doctor John was not entirely happy.

Openings

There are often two openings for a major hotel, the first day of operations, and the official or grand opening. The resort opened for business on November 15, 1988. As usual, this occasion was somewhat of an anticlimax. Apart from local media, sightseers and a minimal number of paying customers, the initial period was rather subdued. This, however, gave the employees some opportunity to settle into their roles.

The Official Opening took place later and was the culmination of a one week opening festival which featured entertainment, fashion, cooking classes, spa indulgence and a Pro Am golf tournament. Given the limited banqueting and conference facilities, on the occasion of the official opening, it was decided to feature a stand up cocktail party for the 300 invited guests, followed by staged dining throughout the resort. The first course was served in The Spa, followed by a course at the Art Centre, with the main course under cover in the village square, and dessert by the main pool. This was quite an ambitious project, and very dependent on benign weather conditions. It was also the wet season with a significant possibility of rain. I was on tenter hooks!

Guests congregated in one of the banquet rooms where cocktails were served, and speeches delivered. They were then invited to proceed to the various food and beverage points. Just as they left the banquet room, the heavens opened. Everyone rushed to the spa and indulged in the first course, under cover. The rain eased, and we managed to coax the congregation to make their way to the Art Centre for the second course. From there it was to the village square for the main course under a marquee. The rain started again and increased to a downpour. I instructed the staff to keep pouring wine hoping that the rain would ease, as the dessert course was outdoors by the pool.

After a protracted period of imbibing fine wines, Chorengal called me to his table and asked what was happening. I explained that I was waiting for a break in the weather. 'To hell with the weather' he said, 'I can't continue to make conversation any longer. Let's go'. So, we announced dessert by the pool and invited the guests to join us. By the pool we had set up the Queensland symphony orchestra under cover, and arranged to have the staff arrive two by two, girl and boy, in black and white tails, with one side of each staff members face painted black, and the other white, to match the tails. They were carrying trays with dessert and champagne.

Much to my delight, and despite my general feelings of alarm over the whole affair, the rain glistened in the spotlights, the orchestra sounded magical, soprano Marina Pryor sounded haunting, the staff looked elegant, and the guests were in awe of what looked like a fairy wonderland. Mind you, they had consumed quite a lot of wine so cared little about the rain. And when I approached our President he whispered 'this is simply beautiful'. I always say, when in doubt, serve more booze.

Operations

After the jamboree of the opening festival, we got down to the business of operating and marketing the resort. This was when reality struck home. Initial occupancy levels were disappointing with costs simply staggering. The layout, concept, and basic inefficient structures produced results that confirmed my worst fears. Monthly losses started to pile up with little respite in sight. I was forced to curtail services. But without a complete change in tack we were destined for serious financial trouble.

I shared my thoughts with both the owning company and Hyatt. I suggested removing the Regency Club designation, closing some lounges, focusing on families and conferences, and opening to the public. There was not much support or enthusiasm for my suggestions, apart from Chorengal telling me to do whatever needed doing.

The first year of operations resulted in a loss of A$6million. I became known as the 6 Million Dollar Man throughout Hyatt. Fortunately or unfortunately, a year later, the Grand Hyatt in Wailea lost US$10millon in its first year, so I lost the infamous mantle.

Experts from all over the place came with advice to help me out of my dilemma. None could offer any bright ideas beyond the strategies I was already applying. It would take time and a lot of hard work.

Some restructuring was necessary in order to accommodate the public and handle larger conferences. One item which required attention was to do with cash registers. There being no regard for serving members of the public in the initial planning, it was considered unnecessary to provide cash registers throughout the resort, as all customers would be resident guests and would charge services to their room account. This reckless oversight resulted in us having to purchase registers, and program them to handle cash and credit cards. In addition, I had a large and permanent marquee erected, suitable to accommodate 600 customers for meetings and meals.

These two examples alone demonstrate the unrealistic nature of the original design. The simple question which must be asked and answered comprehensively relative to any hotel or resort development is ' who are you building it for'? In other words, have you researched and identified the market, or are you simply going on gut feeling. Unfortunately, it is not a case of 'if you build it they will come'.

I am pleased to state that the third year of operations resulted in a breakeven and the resort made an operating profit for a number of years thereafter. I left the resort after an initial period of ten years and for the final year of my tenure the result was an operating profit of A$3.4million. This level of return was miniscule compared to the investment on the part of the owning company, but it was the best that could be done, given the nature of the facility. And it was quite a turnaround!

Kumagai Gumi

As I stated previously, Japanese companies were being encouraged by their government to embark on offshore investments. Rivers of funds flowed from Japan into projects all over the world. There were almost no questions asked as to the viability of projects, or the relevance of feasibility studies. One quite eloquent Japanese investor, Bungo Ishizaki, very succinctly described the environment of the time when he said ' The Japanese banks offered us a window of opportunity, and man did we jump through it'.

When the various projects in Australia belonging to Kumagai reached the operating stage, and most were found to be uneconomical, the company moved to offload them. They sold hotels in Canberra, Hobart and Sydney as well as shopping plazas in Melboure and Perth. They made no effort to sell Coolum despite the mounting losses. This intrigued me. There was very little upside for them in the project, and despite many offers from various investors, there was no inclination to sell. One interaction which I had with the owners representative, was quite puzzling. I advised him of some capital projects which I was embarking on and asked him about funding. He stated that I could spend any operating profits, but that I was not, under any circumstances, to ask him to seek funding from Tokyo. This made me wonder. It was not until my imminent departure from the resort that I received an explanation. I met a gentleman, who had been Doctor Tickell's partner at the early stages. I indicated to him my curiosity relative to the Kumagai position. To my astonishment, he said that the problem related to the fact that the resort did not exist on the books of Kumagai in Tokyo. The project had been funded by money from the Marcos regime in the Philippines. 'The resort does not exist' he said, 'so it is very difficult to justify requests for funds'. This intrigued me further but explained why various delegations of businessmen, who had travelled to Tokyo to make an offer, were treated politely but received no further communication. In the end, the Japanese government embarked on some house cleaning, and instructed companies to clean out any skeletons which might exist from former investments. This proved to be the right place at the right time for the Lend Lease Corporation, who managed to transact a deal to purchase the resort.

Villa Owners

As mentioned previously, the owning company had developed an investment scheme, where individuals could purchase part of or a whole villa, and have it managed by

Hyatt in a letting pool. Essentially, the title to each villa was structured in quarter shares, so any one villa could be owned in quarters by four investors. Or half, or whole. This scheme was only partly successful as only 55% of the villas were sold. This left the owning company with 45%, which was by no means the original intention. This created a dilemma as it was never intended that the owning company would retain such a large share, and thereby significant control in terms of voting rights. The situation was not entirely in keeping with the regulations governing such developments.

Most of the investors bought their shares for reasons of life style. They loved the resort, enjoyed significant discounts when they stayed there, and were not really seeking to make capital gains. All most of them wanted was a nice place to spend their family holidays, and some recognition as investors. Most were well to do.

Some conflict developed, however, as the Hyatt management contract bestowed on Hyatt the absolute right to manage the resort in accordance with international standards of hotel keeping. Hyatt set room rates, controlled room and villa reservations, and was charged with extracting the best return possible from the operation. Hyatt was also incentivised in this regard with a share of any operating profit. This being the case, it was not in Hyatt's interest to have villa owners booking villas at busy times on significantly discounted rates. The rate set for investors was based on the cleaning cost of a villa. Hardly a viable or commercial return.

This situation led to friction when the villa owners realised that they could not make bookings for traditional busy periods like Christmas and Easter holidays. Eventually it was agreed between the parties that Hyatt would reserve a limited number of villas each holiday period for the villa owners. This did not placate everyone, but it was the best compromise.

Golf

Given the quality of the resort golf course, golf became a very significant aspect of the operation. Initially, by way of promoting the resort and the destination, we featured some interesting skins matches. This is a format where the contestants play each hole for a set amount of prize money. The first such match featured Ian Baker Finch, Peter Senior, Craig Parry and Roger Davis. In fact, I believe this was the first time Ian Baker Finch was paid appearance money, it being prior to his British Open win.

Another skins game featured Fred Couples, Larry Mize and Senior and Davis. The two Americans were guaranteed significant appearance money.

We then embarked on developing a tournament on the Australian golf circuit, the Coolum Classic, which became a very popular event for the professional golfers and their families. So popular in fact, that visiting pros from overseas used to say that they had heard about the tournament from their Australian colleagues playing the tours in Europe or the US. It had been described by the pros as a 'must play' if you are touring Australia. The attractive feature of the Coolum Classic was that it was a Pro Am where an amateur played with a pro for the first three days, and then pros played the fourth and final day for the prize money.

It being amateurs and pros and held just prior to Christmas as the last tournament of the year, the atmosphere was holiday and party time. Everyone stayed at the resort, and both amateurs and pros brought their families. It was a really great week of fun, with some serious golf thrown in. In fact, one Australian pro said to me once that when he was discussing his next years schedule with his wife, she said, 'I don't mind where you play, as long as you play Coolum'. Noted golfers I recall playing the event included Ian Baker Finch, Peter Senior, John Senden, Robert Allenby, David Feherty, Jean Van De Velde, and the great Payne Stewart who won the event with tennis champion Todd Woodbridge as his partner.

The Coolum Classic morphed into the Australian PGA Tournament, which is of course a very prestigious tournament on the Australian golfing calendar. While the PGA is a much more serious event commanding greater prize money and pre-eminence, the atmosphere was similar to the Coolum Classic, with pros relaxing with their families on the beach or one of the resort pools. And not a few took to the surf as we had many keen surfers among the golfers. The PGA featured many international stars of golf including Greg Norman, Darren Clarke, Ricky Fowler, Bubba Watson, Brandt Snedeker, Adam Scott and the inimitable John Daly, who threw his putter into the lake on the final hole having had a rather uninspiring round. The putter was fished out some time later and mounted in a glass case in the bar, with appropriate inscription.

The Masters

The Masters is perhaps the pre-eminent golf tournament in all the world. Held in Augusta, Georgia, it is the dream of many golf fans to be there and witness this wonderful event. One of my trips to headquarters in Chicago coincided with the dates of The Masters. During my visit I was contacted by Tony Buffler, a prominent, affable and outstanding golf executive, inviting me to be his guest at the event. I scrambled to arrange flights and managed to arrive in Augusta on a Saturday at 12 midnight.

I asked a taxi driver to find me a room and he replied 'do you know what is going on here right now? You'll be lucky to find any sort of accommodation in this town'. Anyway, we traversed the town and enquired of hotels and motels. Nothing available! Eventually we found a rather dubious motel where an equally dubious night manager was standing behind reception. I asked if he had a room. 'Just one room left' he said, 'and it will cost you $250'. This despite the fact that there was a sign on reception quoting rooms at $25.

But it was this or sleep on a park bench so I took his offer, paid the $250 in cash, and secured a bed in a rather shabby motel room. I slept for a very short five hours, but at least I was somewhat refreshed and ready for a wonderful day of tramping the beautiful fairways of Augusta National Golf Club. This was a very nice bonus from my trip to Chicago.

Tennis

The resort featured an outstanding tennis complex with seven courts, including a stadium type centre court. The tennis coach, Gavin Yarrow, was quite the exuberant personality who infected everyone with his enthusiasm for the game. Gavin was particularly interested in developing up and coming youngsters and seemed to have endless patience imparting the finer points.

One of his charges was a young man named Pat Rafter. Gavin felt that Rafter had that critical X factor which would take him to great heights. How right he was! Pat went on to win two grand slams and many more titles.

I recall a discussion where Gavin was suggesting that the resort offer Pat some sponsorship. This was a very serious decision as the amount involved was $602 in the form of hats and shirts. I scribbled a magnanimous approval on the minutes of the said meeting! The memo introducing the discussions is presented herewith. What a weighty decision that was!

M. Holland

HYATT REGENCY ⊕ COOLUM

HYATT REGENCY COOLUM
PO BOX 78
COOLUM BEACH
QUEENSLAND 4573
TELEPHONE (071) 462 777
TELEFAX (071) 462 957

MEMORANDUM

TO: Melanie Muir
　　　Ian Dearmer
　　cc Exco
　　　Gavin Yarow

FROM: Mark Holland

DATE: 27 August 1990

SUBJECT: **PAT RAFTER**

As you may know Gavin Yarrow has been teaching Pat Rafter, local tennis player ranked Number 1 in Queensland U18 and Number 2 in Australia U18.

Hyatt Regency Coolum would like to sponsor Pat by way of the following:-

(i)　Providing a suitable amount of Hyatt Regency Coolum sportwear. The amounts agreed are:-

T-Shirts	20 @ $14	$280
Caps	10 @ $ 6	$ 60
Racket Covers	4 @ $16	$ 64
Sweatshirts	6 @ $33	$198
TOTAL		$602

(ii)　Allowing Pat the complimentary use of the recreation facilities within the Resort. Normal charges will apply on personal services will apply.

(iii)　When conducting clinics in the Resort, accommodation, including breakfast, will be provided.

(iv)　Use of the centre court at predetermined times to practice.

In return Pat agrees to:-
(i)　Pat agrees to promote Hyatt Regency Coolum at all times and to wear Hyatt Regency Coolum logo gear during practice and off court during all tennis

OK

Promotions and Personalities.

In an ongoing effort to lift the profile of the resort and establish it as a destination, we embarked on a number of major events in the form of concerts, wine seminars, rugby and Australian Rules football. We featured a major concert with Michael Crawford, the star of Phantom of The Opera, and we had an attendance of 7000 fans.

This particular event proved to be exceedingly stressful due to that least reliable of all factors, the weather. Once again it was to be the bane of my life at Coolum. The concert was an outdoor event on the golf practice range. During the setup of the stage and seating the weather turned foul with flooding rain and howling wind. The forecast was not encouraging. The local media interviewed me and suggested that we cancel and refund the tickets. I jokingly replied that I would prove that God is an Irishman, and that it would not rain for the concert.

Most people said I was mad, including the promoter of the concert, who gave me until the morning of the event at 9am to make a final decision. That deadline was last minute as he and his team had a mountain of work to complete if we were going ahead. We met at the appointed hour with the sky full of clouds and the winds whistling over the practice range. What was my decision? This was a rather scary moment. It was entirely my decision. Cancel the event and refund the tickets, and avoid possible mayhem if we were to proceed and be washed out? Or take a chance.

I decided to take a chance and hope for the luck of the Irish. We went ahead, and in the early afternoon we had a promising break in the weather. The seats filled, the darkness arrived, the lights went up and Michael Crawford and his daughter delivered the most wonderful concert one could imagine. I, however, spent the whole evening on tenterhooks worrying about the weather. Since I could'nt see the sky, I had no idea if it was clear or about to deliver a deluge. The concert ended to huge acclaim from the audience. I went back stage to congratulate the stars, and as I was chatting to them, the heavens opened and down came the rain. Yes, God is an Irishman!

The Wine Guru

Len Evans was what some describe as the God Father of the Australian wine industry. He was an ebullient character full of energy, and totally committed to ensuring that Australian wine gained recognition for quality throughout the world. I became friendly with Len and here is how it happened.

Always searching for ways to promote the resort, we embarked on setting up a wine exposition where wine lovers could learn from the experts, taste great wines, and have fun. Through some coaxing, Len agreed to participate and this provided a certain fillip to the event. Having Len resulted in other wine personalities taking part and lent great credibility to the whole affair. Over time we had the pleasure of the company of Brian Croser, James Halliday and Jancis Robinson from the BBC, to name a few.

On the initial occasion, when Len was about to check into the resort, I wondered what welcome item to place in his room. I decided against wine, for I knew that Len was a rather frank individual and that if he did not like my choice, he would have no hesitation in publicly lambasting me for it. Instead, I rather stupidly decided to send him a very nice fruit display. That evening, we had an introductory dinner for all the wine makers and Len was asked to say some words. He was very supportive of the wine event and said some encouraging things. However, he noted that when he stayed at a decent hotel like a Sheraton or a Westin, he was usually welcomed with a bottle of Krug or, at the very least, Dom Perignon champagne. At the Hyatt Coolum he said, 'this miserable Irishman sent me an apple and an orange'. Of course, this was all said in jest, but it was embarrassing all the same.

The following evening we again had a dinner but a much more formal and lavish affair. Len again rose to say some words to a much larger audience, and again referred to the 'miserable Irishman' and his apple and orange. Well, not to be outdone, I contacted one of my managers and asked him to place a dozen Dom Perignon in Len's room, anywhere he saw fit.

Next morning Len and I were playing golf and he says to me 'you bastard, when I got back to my room last night there was a bottle of Dom Perignon on the table with no ice bucket, and at room temperature. I thought what a pathetic gesture! When I went to go to the toilet there were two bottles sticking out of the toilet. I opened the TV cabinet and there were bottles sticking out of that. And when I got into bed there were bottles in the bed. I decided to get up and round up all the bottles, but I could only find 11. I knew there must be a 12th. I searched on my hands and knees all over the room but could not find the missing bottle'. I loved it! I was just imaging Len full of good wine searching all over the room in his underwear and being frustrated. "Anyway', he said 'how many can I keep'. I said you can keep one, but you will have to share it with me, which we did after golf.

One day, Len asked me if I could cook. I said I could and that I would like to have him to dinner at my house. He said he liked 'wet food' and I advised him that I did a very nice French chicken fricassee, which I thought he'd like. Well, he loved it, and mopped up the sauce with his bread roll. Not only that, but the lady sitting next to him, who he didn't know, was a small eater and had not finished her meal. Len enquired if she was not going to eat what was left on her plate and she said she'd had enough. Without a pause, Len reached over and took her plate. He then wolfed down what the lady had left behind. She wasn't very impressed, but I thought it was hilarious, and what a compliment to my cooking.

We became good friends with Len and his lovely wife Trish. They returned to the resort on a number of occasions, and Cathie and I had the pleasure of staying with them in their wonderful house in the Hunter Valley.

Len had contributed greatly to the success of the wine event which became a significant annual attraction for most of the Australian wine industry, and attracted thousands of Sunshine Coast residents. Len's support role was taken on by Geoff Merrill, a good friend, outstanding winemaker, and bon vivant.

The Rolling Stones

Many personalities passed through Coolum but none greater than the Rolling Stones. The Stones were appearing in Brisbane as part of the world Voodoo Lounge Tour in 1995. They had a very large entourage, including wives and family, tutors for children, security and technical crew. All up approximately 100 people. They decided to take time out in Queensland, and sought accommodation that was secure, convenient to Brisbane, and suitable for a group with diverse interests. Someone recommended the Hyatt Coolum and we were approached. We were obviously excited at the prospect and conscious of the publicity this would generate, not only for the resort but for the Sunshine Coast destination. While I had some misgivings that they might only be making enquiries, I was surprised when the booking was confirmed, and we were about to welcome The Stones.

The entourage arrived and were ensconced in appropriate accommodation. Mick Jagger, Keith Richards, Ronnie Wood and Charlie Watt occupied villas in the Ambassador area, with the rest of the crew in lakeside villas. The lovely Jerry Hall accompanied Jagger.

It was very noticeable that Mick Jagger had a very strict diet and exercise regime. He did not drink alcohol, and spent many hours working out in the gym. This was not surprising, considering the energetic performance he delivers on stage.

There was a very significant buzz in the local community when word of the band's stay at the resort became public.

The manager of the tour provided us with pseudonyms for each member of the band, with instructions not to accept calls from anyone making enquiries in their real names. Genuine friends and acquaintances would be provided with the pseudonyms, and would ask for those. It was amazing how many calls and letters we received for the group. Literally hundreds of letters asking for money, inviting them to parties or simply gushing with adoration were received and discarded.

A number of memorable incidents occurred during their stay. On one occasion they asked us to arrange a beach party, and requested that we provide a band. Obviously, we were not to advise the local band who the client was. So, we hired a group of local rockers to provide the music at the resort beach club. For fun, the four Stones hid in the bushes and did not appear until the band was in full swing. Then out of the bushes came the Rolling Stones. Well, our local rockers almost wet themselves. And the Stones even jammed with them, something they'll probably reminisce about forever.

On another occasion, some early morning golfers were playing the 11th hole at the resort, which is a short par three over water. When they got to the tee, there was a body spreadeagled on the green. The golfers proceeded to play and hit their balls onto the green, obviously avoiding the human obstruction. When they got to the green they realised the sleeping apparition was Keith Richards. It must've been a big night!

The Boss's Romance

The Hyatt President, Bernd Chorengal, decided that Coolum should host the Hyatt Asia Pacific General Managers Meeting. This is always a very stressful undertaking for the unfortunate manager of the chosen hotel. Apart from having to look after the host of Hyatt senior executives, the hotel is reviewed by a most critical audience of fellow general managers. This is not an experience sought after by many managers. In any case, Coolum became the host and we managed to pass muster! But the meeting gave rise to an interesting life changing event.

Chorengal was, of course, lodged in the upmarket Ambassador section of the resort with private villa, swimming pool and guest lounge. Employed as a concierge in the guest lounge was a comely young lady called Sharon, who hailed from the beachside suburb of Noosa. Sharon was a striking and convivial young woman, and she greatly impressed the President. So much so, that Chorengal came to my office the day before departure and said that he had a problem! I was somewhat perplexed wondering what it could be!

He said that he had invited the lovely Sharon to join him on his onward journey, and she had accepted. 'Well' I said, 'I suppose I'll have to change the roster'. Sharon departed the next day with the President in a helicopter bound for Sanctuary Cove resort, another Hyatt further down the coast. The happy couple then continued on to Chicago and, low and behold, they were married some time later.

As much as I wished them every happiness, I was conscious that this development could result in frequent visits to Coolum. Naturally, Sharon liked to return to visit her family at Christmas, and I was therefore confronted with having the President of Hyatt as a guest for a number of weeks, and on a regular basis! And Chorengal was not one to switch off. On many occasions, he would ask me to join him for a drink and discussion. So I spent many interesting evenings drinking wine until the wee small hours, listening to him. Then I had to get up in the morning and do a day's work, while my boss slept until midday. My colleagues in Hyatt resorts around the world were delighted, and relieved, that they did not have to suffer a similar fate. They were off the hook. Coolum became the boss' Christmas destination.

Berlin

I was very actively involved in promoting the resort both domestically and internationally. This took me on journeys to Sydney, Melbourne, Tokyo, Chicago and Berlin. Berlin, in particular, hosts the largest travel show in Europe, where the international travel industry gather to exchange ideas, review product and do deals. It is a world renowned show, with decision makers of airlines, travel agents, hotels, developers, and a myriad of other travel related enterprises taking part.

My trip to this event coincided with the collapse of the Berlin Wall. This was a historical and quite earth shattering event. After years of servitude to a corrupt and harsh regime, East German people were suddenly allowed to cross over to the West. The feeling in what was then West Berlin was simply euphoric. After 40 years, the cold war had ended, and this monstrosity dividing their city was coming down. Berliners were overjoyed.

East Berliners flocked to the West and were astonished to find the sheer abundance of food and other goods in retail outlets. Those who visited the KaDeWe supermarket actually thought that the mountains of fresh produce on display had been put there only to impress those poor souls coming from the East. They said that so much food could never be sold and would go rotten. This was indicative of the horrific conditions these individuals had coped with for generations. They were so used to scarcity that they could'nt believe such abundance was normal.

A great friend, Richard White, and I actually crossed over into the East. We were shocked at the almost derelict conditions. Buildings which had suffered bomb damage in the Second World War had'nt been repaired. The few shops featured almost nothing in window displays. People seemed to be in a state of fear. What may seem like a minor detail, but impressed upon me the horrible uniformity of the communist system, was that all the cars were the same colour and make - grey box shaped Russian built Ladas. The disparity between East and West Berlin was simply astonishing.

My Family

My family and I lived in a very comfortable four bedroom house on the resort. As my wife used to say, we were far enough away for privacy, but close enough for room service! The house was surrounded by gardens, with a rather large undeveloped piece of resort land adjoining. We had a cat, a dog, a budgie, and my daughter, Sarah, even had a horse, which we kept in the adjoining field. In essence, and unlike most hotel managers who lived in hotel flats, we lived as normal people with a separate access, meaning we could come and go without entering or leaving through the main resort entrance. This was a rather pleasant bonus.

Of course, we all had the use of all the resort amenities including swimming pools, tennis courts, art centre, bicycles, beach and even the spa. So all in all life was pretty good. Our children, Sean, Sarah and Emma, all went to boarding schools in Brisbane. However, it was weekly boarding so they came home to Coolum most weekends. Like most kids, they'd invite fellow boarders home for a sleepover. Of course, their house guests were somewhat taken aback when they realised that the sleepover was at the Hyatt with all its wonderful facilities. Invitations from the Holland kids were keenly accepted!

We were also blessed to have Ernie. Ernie was a very affable and kind kitchen hand who was always there when the Hollands needed help. Ernie would clean and set up the barbecue, move tables, brush yards and generally see to it that the external areas of the general managers residence were in tip top shape for the reception of guests. My children used to refer to Ernie as the 'fix it man', regardless of the issue at hand. In fact, I once heard my son in law, Geoff, say to my daughter Sarah, 'you know what, we need an Ernie". Everybody does.

Hawaii

My family and I visited Hawaii and stayed at the Hyatt Regency Maui. This hotel was developed by the illustrious Chris Hemmeter who was a very prominent figure in the islands and a major player in resort development. Hemmeter's family owned a small shop in a shopping strip on Waikiki Beach. Chris got to thinking that the strip represented a magnificent development site if he could convince the owners of the other shops to allow him to explore the possibilities. All the owners agreed and gave him an option on their holding. So, he now had control over a very significant piece of land right on the beach. He approached various developers and was successful in completing a deal for the sale of the entire strip. The owners of these little tourist shops were delighted and gladly signed up. Today the 1200 room Hyatt Waikiki Beach stands on the site.

Hemmeter went on to develop other resorts including the Hyatt Regency Maui where he lived for quite some time in a palatial suite. At the time of our visit Hemmeter had sold the hotel and moved out. For fun, the General Manager, Werner, decided to allocate the Hemmeter suite to the Holland family. What fun we had. The suite was so large that it featured an ornamental lake with swans floating graciously. There were four beautifully appointed bedrooms with gold plated taps in all the bathrooms.

The fun, however, was based around the fact that we were given a key to this extravagant oasis with a simple room number written on it. So, each time we would order something in the restaurant or by the pool we would give the room number to be told by the staff that there was no such number. We would pretend innocence and say that this is the number we were given. Then after some investigation the staff would realise that we were in the Hemmeter Suite and the reaction was amazing. They did not know who we were but we must surely be some important people if we were in the Hemmeter Suite. We were feted as VIPs.

New Delhi, No.

Despite my absolute commitment to Coolum, and the many wonderful times my family and I enjoyed there, I was starting to develop itchy feet. This was 1998, and I had spent ten years at the resort. I felt that it was time to move on and indicated this to President Chorengal in one of our many conversations. He asked me where I thought I would like to go next and I simply suggested a 'world city'. Tokyo, New York, London, wherever, but I felt that I needed, and could handle, a large project in a major metropolis.

Chorengal noted my aspirations and said he would keep them in mind. Some months later I received a call from Hyatt headquarters in Chicago asking me if I would consider going to open the Grand Hyatt in New Delhi. Obviously, Chorengal was true to his word, so I eagerly accepted the challenge.

However, I was dealing with one of Chorengal's lieutenants, a certain Rakesh Sarna, who was a vice president. Sarna and I discussed the project and the conditions of my employment. I was simply aghast at how low the salary offer was, and indicated to him that it was significantly less than I was receiving in Coolum, even though it was tax free. In addition,

I was prepared to leave my daughter in boarding school in Brisbane, which would save the hotel owning company the cost of school fees. My older children were now at university!

Sarna said he would give the matter some thought and get back to me. He responded some time later saying that he felt that I should take my daughter to India with me, which would save me school fees in Brisbane, but he had no discretion to increase the salary.

This was disappointing, but I said I would consider it. Not more than a couple of weeks later I received a regular bulletin from Hyatt Chicago which, among other things, announced the appointment of the general manager for the new Grand Hyatt in New Delhi. I was flabbergasted! I had received no further communication. I had not refused the position, and was simply ignored. This made me mad!

I suppose I had simply experienced some of the poison that afflicts the corporate world. As it turned out though, the Grand Hyatt New Delhi became a very difficult proposition for Hyatt. The owner of the hotel was extremely difficult to deal with and quite duplicitous in his dealings. After many months of confrontation, Hyatt withdrew from the management contract. Perhaps I was better off in the end.

Sydney 2000 Olympic Games

During my time at Coolum I became friendly with a number of interesting and high profile people. One was Graham Richardson, a Senator and cabinet minister in the national government. Richo, as he is known, was also a heavyweight in the Australian Labor party and was often referred to as the 'numbers man'. He was instrumental in having leaders appointed and removed! Graham is a very intelligent, personable, and Machiavellian character. "Whatever it Takes" is the title of his book on politics!

He became a regular visitor to Coolum, and we played some golf together. Our families dined together and generally we had some good times. Just around the time of my New Delhi debacle Graham asked me how long I was going to stay at Coolum. I replied that I was in fact developing itchy feet. That I felt it was time to move on. Well, be careful what you say and what you wish for.

Some weeks later I had a call from a certain Jim Sloman, the chief operating officer for the Sydney 2000 Olympic Games. Jim introduced himself as a friend of Richo, and I initially thought he was calling seeking a discount, as friends of friends used to do! However, Sloman said that he heard that I was exploring the possibility of a new challenge, and that he felt he had the exact job for me. General Manager of the Olympic Athletes Village!

Well, I was somewhat taken aback and replied that I was in fact considering my position, but that the Sydney Olympics was not where I saw my next move. Jim asked me to at least come down to Sydney to meet him and have a chat. 'These kind of chats can get a fellow into trouble', I said, 'but okay I will make the trip but no promises'. I was unaware at this stage that Richo was involved with the organising committee, and was designated to be the Mayor of The Athletes Village.

I met Jim in Sydney along with John Coates, the President of the Australian Olympic Committee, and the man credited with almost single handedly securing the games for Sydney. The enormous scope of the project was explained to me, along with the need to establish not only the Athletes Village for 16,000 inhabitants, but a Media Village for 6000 media, and various other smaller villages for games officials. The simple fact was that at that time, Sydney did not have enough hotel rooms to accommodate the travelling circus! I suggested that in terms of operational synergy, all these village projects should be managed as one unit, under a competent executive. My interviewers agreed with this suggestion and challenged me to take on the entire project.

I returned home to Coolum with misgivings about taking on a role which, while exciting, was short term. I had a career with Hyatt, even though I was continually frustrated with the organisation. And, above all, I was a hotelier. It seemed that I would be making a reckless decision to terminate my relationship with Hyatt for a role that had dubious future prospects. I recall the awful soul searching I went through trying to decide.

My children were at university and on their way in life. We had enjoyed Coolum but perhaps it was time. Neither my wife or I enjoyed living in Asia, which is where a next move with Hyatt would probably eventuate. In the midst of my anxious considerations my daughter Sarah said to me, 'Dad, this is the Sydney 2000 Olympic Games. What a thrill to be part of that'. Well, out of the mouths of babes, as the saying goes. Yes, I would like to be part of it. Why not?

So, much to the surprise of my boss, I tendered my resignation with Hyatt. Since our children were at university in Brisbane, we decided to purchase a home there, and for me to commute on a weekly basis to Sydney. The Olympic committee agreed to this arrangement as they could contra my airfares with Ansett Airlines, who were a major sponsor.

International Olympic Committee

I was surprised at the limited knowledge which the IOC seemed to have accumulated regarding games operations, and, in particular, the operational set up of the village. They had lots of information on the eligibility of teams, their entitlements in terms of accommodation, and the qualifying of athletes, but in terms of operational knowhow there was simply no advice. Operational expertise tended to be garnered from people who had worked on previous games, and as Atlanta preceded Sydney, a number of Atlanta stalwarts were recruited to provide knowledge and guidance. While these individuals were very helpful, their experience in the Atlanta Athletes Village was not a pleasant one, as there were many operational problems and lots of disgruntled athletes. Despite this, their assistance was valuable, for it helped us to avoid a similar catastrophe, as they taught us what not to do.

In addition, there was the imponderable issue of estimating the number of athletes who would qualify. Somehow the IOC could not categorically estimate the final number as qualifications continued right up until the opening day of the village. All they could do was give a best estimate, and seemingly this was the issue which undid the preparations in Atlanta. The Atlanta village underestimated the final numbers and did not have sufficient beds. A pretty unfortunate start. In fact, one of the Atlanta managers gave me some sound advice. He said, 'whatever you do, bunk the beds' because that would alleviate the pressure if the numbers turn out to be greater than the IOC estimate. Despite protestations from IOC representatives, I decided to bunk the beds and was very glad that I did so, as the number of athletes was considerably greater than estimated.

Operations

My immediate impression was that I was on my own, and simply had to establish a team that would deliver the best possible outcomes. This team became known as the Village People for obvious reasons, and one of my first appointments was my personal assistant from Coolum, Anne Callanan, who enthusiastically joined the team. This was of course a boon to me having Anne by my side. I then set about recruiting food and beverage management, housekeeping, accommodation managers, and others.

Traditionally, the games are manned by a host of volunteers. The Sydney volunteers were simply wonderful people, who gave of their time to play a role in making visitors feel welcome in their wonderful city. In the Athletes Village we had 2000 volunteers working around the clock looking after the athletes.

The Village was located at Homebush, quite close to the Olympic Stadium. It was essentially a new housing development, with the houses converted to accommodate up to 12 athletes, sharing two to a room, with the garage converted to a bedroom, and additional toilet and shower facilities added in temporary structures. In addition, a number of demountable units were put in place as there were'nt sufficient houses to accommodate all the residents.

Teams were entitled to so many beds based on the number of qualified athletes, and it became clear that a number of the larger teams were used to horse trading beds for extra space. Teams like the US, Germany, Great Britain and such had entitlement to so many beds, but did not require all of them, as some of their athletes would stay in hotels or elsewhere, depending on their sport. These teams would offer to trade their extra beds for additional space like massage rooms, meeting rooms and the like. As the village was fully booked and there was always the chance that extra athletes would qualify over and above the IOC estimate, the Village management was happy to trade and garner the extra beds.

The Athletes Village consisted of accommodation for 16,000 athletes and officials, a dining room that seated 5000, a 500 seat stand alone grill restaurant, a medical facility, spa, retail outlets, post office, bank, coffee stations, an amphitheatre, and an ongoing entertainment program featuring buskers, magicians, acrobats and the like. The medical facility was state of the art and even made condoms available to the athletes. These very important medical safeguards were freely available from a rather large glass bowl on the reception desk for athletes to help themselves. And they did. I was led to believe that a total of 34,000 condoms were distributed. The age of free love!

The food operation was managed by Spotless Catering and the head chef, Peter Wright, was an outstanding production manager. In the main dining hall a significant amount of the dishes were prepared on demand. All manner of international food was featured including Western, Japanese, Thai, Indian, Malay, Korean, Italian, and Kocher. We even had a McDonalds restaurant as Maccas was, and is, a major sponsor. Pasta was cooked to order, as well as pizzas. The buffets were lavish and the athletes delighted in the food. I recall standing in the main dining room with our Food and Beverage Manager, Anto Sweetapple, and the room was almost full of athletes from all over the world. After all our preparations and stress we looked at each other and said, 'we've done it, we are feeding almost 5000 of the worlds athletes without a problem'. What a great feeling it was.

Israel Team

The Chef de Mission or leader of the Israeli team came to my office one day prior to the games, and asked me if we intended to feature Kocher food in the village. I told him that it was not my intention to do so as Kocher food was very expensive, and I did not have the budget. He was very disappointed and said that he would have difficulty advising his Olympic Committee that there would be no Kocher food. Would I reconsider. I understood his dilemma but could not oblige. A few days later he invited me to dinner in a rather luxurious home of his friends in Dover Heights. The dinner party was a casual stand up affair with approximately thirty people present. We had a pleasant evening and then, almost in unison, the dinner guests set out to cajole me into providing Kocher food. They were quite humorous about the whole issue but keen to get their way. I said I would review the matter. One of the guests actually said to me 'nobody will eat the shit, but we have to have it'. So, I gave in and ordered a very limited amount. And the dinner guest was right, nobody did eat the shit!

The Israel team was housed in a section of the village surrounded by teams whose countries had no issue with Israel. Their team quarters were surrounded by a brush type fence with permanent guards stationed on the perimeter. The Olympic policy is that no team could carry firearms or have armed guards in the village. Whether the guards of the complex were armed or not I do not know, but considering what occurred at the Munich 1972 village, I would not be surprised if they were. I did not enquire!

Rich and Poor

Teams from the major countries tended to be lavishly kitted out with the latest sporting equipment and designer uniforms. In addition, they were accompanied by professional coaches, masseurs, doctors, and sports psychologists. These teams also, of course, included some of the greatest athletes in the world. All were trained to peak condition.

On the other hand there were some teams who came from poorer nations and simply did not have the funds for equipment and resources. A rather sad but uplifting aspect of this disparity relates to the team from the new nation of East Timor. The athletes from this months old country arrived carrying their belongings in shopping bags, with absolutely no equipment whatsoever.

When they arrived at the village welcome area, the police manning the security decided they must do something to help these athletes. So, they arranged to provide the East Timor team with sports shoes, track suits, and even formal made to measure suits for them to wear in the opening ceremony parade. What a great gesture. I can still see the smiles on the East Timor athletes as they walked around the stadium in the parade, wearing their very bespoke business suits.

Welcome Ceremonies.

Graham Richardson was the Mayor of the Village. This is a honorary position, but Richo was a very active and involved mayor. Fortunately, he and I were on friendly terms from my time at Coolum, and we got along well together. I respected and appreciated Graham's input and he was generally very helpful and totally committed to the welfare of the athletes. He was briefed on all aspects of the operation, and was determined to ensure that the village was a success.

Graham, along with the Deputy Mayor, Sallyanne Atkinson, one time mayor of Brisbane, conducted the welcoming ceremonies for the teams. The ceremony included welcome speeches, exchange of gifts, and a children's choir singing a lovely specially written welcome song. The ceremony for each team was held in the village amphitheatre which was located quite close to some of the housing units. So close in fact, that some of the team leaders refused to have their teams located close to the amphitheatre, as the music might disturb their athletes.

I was worried as to which team I could convince to accept this particular accommodation. I need not have worried though, for when the Cuban team leader was advised of what was going on in the amphitheatre, he immediately said that is where he would like his team to be housed. 'We Cubans love music' he said, And they certainly did. On many occasions when the welcome song was being sung by the choir, there were Cuban athletes on their balconies joining in the chorus.

On one occasion I received a report that the tennis coach of the team from Kazakstan had disappeared. He had been missing for a couple of days with no trace. I brought this to Richo's attention. He said 'Which team'. I said Kazakstan, to which Richo responded 'lets see how high that rates on the who gives a fuck Richter scale'. Perhaps if it had been the US, Germany, UK or any one of the more prominent teams, our Mayor would have responded more appropriately!

Richo was very intent on featuring an Australian food item on the village menu. The ubiquitous meat pie! He even went so far as to have a blind pie tasting to choose the right one. He also visited pie shops in his search for the best. I, unfortunately, advised him of a famous pie shop which I thought he should try. I was not very familiar with Sydney, and told him the shop was in Chatswood. After some time driving around Chatswood searching for the pie shop he called and berated me saying 'the shop is in North Sydney, you stupid Irish bastard. I have been driving around asking people where the shop was and they tell me I am in the wrong bloody suburb'. I could not help laughing at the vision of the rather well known and quite corpulent Richo, asking people the whereabouts of a pie shop.

Opening Ceremony

The logistics surrounding the Opening Ceremony are enormous, intricate, and challenging. Here is an event where the host city is on show and the world is watching. From the village perspective, our job was to coordinate the transfer of 16,000 athletes and officials by bus from the village to the stadium and back again. This was no easy task as the teams had to be moved in a particular order relative to their place in the parade.

There was also the very major consideration of security, especially on the return. But we managed to pull it off without a hitch, and as most of the athletes decided to walk back we had a very orderly re-entry through security.

Just prior to the ceremony, I was advised that one of the major teams actually had double the number of tickets they required for the occasion. Seemingly, the team sponsor had bought tickets for the team and the organising committee had also allocated tickets. It was important that the seats be filled, as they were prominent in the stadium which was fully booked and empty seats would not have been a good look! We decided to issue the tickets to staff members and volunteers who had worked the early shift and wished to attend. In addition, I contacted my family in Brisbane and told them to jump on a plane as we had tickets to the ceremony. My wife says she never moved so fast! So there we were, practically in the front row witnessing what was quite a wonderful occasion.

Visiting Personalities

The village was visited by representatives of practically every government which had diplomatic relations with Australia. Diplomats came to encourage their country's athletes. The US was represented by Chelsea Clinton, daughter of the President. The greatest boxer of all time, Mohammad Ali, also visited and was enthusiastically greeted by team members. What a beautiful gentle giant was this man, with quite a quirky sense of humour.

The most moving visit was that by Nelson Mandela, former President of South Africa. When Mandela arrived at the South African team quarters the athletes, black and white, linked arms on both sides of the walkway as Mandela walked through. Many of the athletes, again both black and white, were in tears of joy at seeing, and being so close to, this great human being. I thought 'this is the new South Africa'. Unfortunately, at time of writing it seems that Mandela's dream of a wholesome, free and democratic country has yet to be realised. This is very sad given the very obvious enthusiasm and pride displayed by the country's young athletes.

The Paralympic Village

With the sad departure of the Olympic teams we had to refocus and prepare for the arrival of the Paralympians. Many aspects of the village had to be retrofitted to accommodate athletes with disabilities. I was very determined that we'd deliver the same level of service to the Paralympians, as we'd done for the Olympians. I needn't have worried.

The staff and volunteers were magnificent in greeting and looking after these disabled athletes. And the athletes were so appreciative of the kindness of the staff that some were just about in tears of joy. To see people with major disabilities getting on with life, and performing for their country, was mind blowing. Their positive attitude was a lesson to all of us.

Media Coverage

One aspect of staging the games was somewhat of a worry – the media. It seems that the media in every host city is determined to identify shortcomings with the organisation. Dire warnings of how incompetent the Sydney Organising Committee was appeared daily in news bulletins. Sydney and Australia were about to be embarrassed by the numbskulls organising the games. It went on and on. So much so, that staff taking a taxi to organising committee headquarters would be lambasted by taxi drivers as fools for working with such an incompetent organisation. Staff actually started denying they were employees, stating that they were simply visiting!

In the end, when the games were pronounced a huge success and the 'best games ever' by Juan Antonio Samaranch, the media turned full circle, and hoorayed the committee and the workers. I also received some letters of gratitude from team leaders who were more than happy with how they were treated in the village. In fact, one team leader wrote to thank me for 'operating the best ever Athletes Village in the best ever Olympic Games'

The Organising Committee

Sydney were the last games held under the reign of IOC President, Antonio Samaranch. The IOC those days was not a particularly efficient organisation. IOC members were feted and expected tickets to every event, and VIP treatment. They were also known not to turn up at most events leaving seats which could be sold, vacant. The number of premium tickets allocated to the members was quite significant, and was a major cost to the organising committee, especially in a city like Sydney where the population is sports mad with tickets to every event in high demand. The organising committee balked at this requirement and refused to allocate tickets. This caused some significant consternation in the IOC ranks but Sydney stuck to their guns.

Another deficiency of the IOC at that time was the complete lack of transferrable knowledge about the games. They simply did not keep records of past games relative to operating guidelines. They were what could be referred to as amateur. This deficiency was corrected by the Sydney organising committee, who developed a huge portfolio on games operations and transferred this to the IOC. I believe that the IOC actually paid a fee of $3 million for this service. I would think it was worthwhile. In this regard, I think it is important to stress that the modern IOC is now a well managed and transparent organisation, committed to assisting host cities in every way possible.

Athens 2004

At the end of the Sydney event I was approached by John Wallis, a Vice President with Hyatt, and a personal friend.

John asked me if I would be prepared to take on the position of General Manager of the Hyatt Regency in Dubai, with the role also overseeing the construction and opening of the Grand Hyatt Dubai, the plan being for me to move to the Grand Hyatt for the opening. I was very grateful and keen to take on the role, as I had missed the hotel business. However, my previous mentor, Andre Pury, also a Vice President, had other ideas. Andre had promised the role to another candidate, so I missed out. This was disappointing but life goes on.

The President of the Athens 2004 Olympic Organising Committee or ATHOC, was a rather glamourous Greek business woman by the name of Gianna Angelopoulos Daskalaki. This lady was quite dynamic and absolutely determined to deliver a successful games for Athens.

There was a story where the Greek media were suggesting that Gianna and her husband were somehow embezzling the organising committee, and were corruptly syphoning off funds. In this regard, her husband was interviewed by a journalist who asked him if he had been a millionaire before or after he married Gianna. The husband replied ' after, before I was a billionaire'. Despite the innuendo, there was no evidence of any wrong doing on the part of Gianna or her husband.

Gianna came to Sydney as a guest and observer and decided that she should have a number of the Sydney managers come to Athens to help with the games. We were invited to a cocktail party to meet her. She went around the room smiling gracefully and saying to particular individuals in her lusty voice, ' I need you to help me'. This was quite flattering for those concerned, but going to Greece was not my intention.

However, the Chief Operating Officer, Jim Sloman, decided to play a role in securing the services of the nominated managers. Jim set up a company and offered his services to Gianna and Athens. It seemed easier for them to work through one organisation than to deal with a group of individuals, so they signed a deal with Jim. As I was on the list of desirables, Jim contacted me and asked me if I was prepared to be involved. I was reluctant, but Jim insisted I visit him to discuss the matter. He could be quite persuasive!

In any case, after some long discussion, I wrote a number on a piece of paper and said that was the salary I would require in order to consider Athens, and it had to be tax free with accommodation and transport provided. I thought, and almost hoped, my demand would not be accepted. However, some weeks later Jim called me to say they'd accepted.

My deal was a strange one. For the first six months I was to spend a month in Athens and then return home to Brisbane for a month, return flights provided. After the six month period, I was to be permanently based in Athens.

Athens is a very historic city, but quite dysfunctional. The world somehow perceives Greece as an ancient country, but as a nation Greece was formed in recent times through some extremely turbulent episodes.

Freedom from the Ottoman Empire in the 1800's resulted in both civil and international strife, and long periods of hardship for the Greek people. Athens became the capital of the new Greek nation and was flooded with Greeks from all over Asia Minor, who were keen to establish themselves in their homeland. The city expanded over the years with very doubtful infrastructure. Roads, sewage, apartment buildings, and parking were never adequately provided resulting in congestion, power failures, and lots of frustration on the part of the inhabitants.

My introduction to the city coincided with the completion of the subway, which led to even more traffic nightmares. This environment of endless stress tended to make the inhabitants of Athens quite aggressive, unlike their fellows in the countryside and on the Greek islands, where life is at a slow and wholesome pace, and the people generous and welcoming.

Greece is a member of the European Union. This association somewhat controls their rather reckless approach to public finances, but not entirely. One story told to me by a certain country's ambassador to Greece sheds some illumination on the Greeks, and the European Union. Citizens of EU countries are entitled to purchase land in any member state. In order to process such purchase it is, of course, necessary that the purchaser receives a valid title to the land.

Unfortunately, Greece never had a comprehensive land survey completed, so establishing title rights was pretty arbitrary. Most title had been in families for generations, and was recognised with landmarks such as large rocks, or the edge of streams and lakes. This of course was not acceptable to the EU.

However, the Greek government pleaded poor saying that they did not have the necessary funds to survey the entire country in order to establish legal title. The EU agreed to fund the project, which was to be addressed with some urgency. A few years later some bureaucrat in EU headquarters in Brussels decided to check on the progress. He sent a delegation to Athens to enquire. The delegation was advised that, despite millions of Euros in funding, and the employment of 16,000 bureaucrats involved in the process, only one title had been recorded! The EU representatives were appalled at the waste of time and money and threatened to stop the funding.

The Greeks responded by saying that if the funding was stopped, then the 16,000 bureaucrats would lose their jobs, and the Greeks would blame this outcome on the EU. This threat somewhat compromised the EU position, so it was agreed that the funding would continue but would be monitored to ensure more robust results.

Athens was awarded the Olympic Games by the Olympic Committee of Antonio Samaranch, a number of whom were later found to be corrupt. It is very doubtful if a city like Athens would ever again be awarded the games, as it simply did not have the fundamental infrastructure necessary to handle such an imposing event. As a result, the games cost the Greek government an inordinate amount of money, which they could ill afford.

The modern IOC would surely only award the games to a city that is already equipped with most of the necessary infrastructure and technology. This most certainly reduces the overall cost.

My role in Athens was as a consultant in terms of reviewing plans, establishing operating guidelines, and liaising with IOC, ATHOC, and visiting country representatives. I also established manning guides. However, in Sydney I took up my position two years out from the games and managed well within that timeframe. In Athens I was in place four years prior to the games which was simply too early. My days were less than full.

In addition, myself and the other Sydney representatives tended to work our normal 8 am to 5pm office hours, while the Greeks regularly arrived at ten or eleven in the morning and stayed until late in the evening. This resulted in somewhat of a miscommunication where the Sydney team became more and more isolated from what was going on. In addition, there was the usual jockeying for position in the organising committee, and some significant bloodletting when a new chief executive, Marton Simitsek, was appointed.

He immediately took aim at the number of consultants which had been retained. In this regard, he was heard to say that ' we Greeks do not need foreigners to show us how to do the job'. Fair enough, I thought, but every games needs input from those who have done it before, and Athens was no exception. Regardless, Simitsek set about reducing the number of highly paid consultants, and my team was included in this review.

I was in Paris with my wife for the weekend, after having lived in Athens on and off for 18 months. I received a call from Jim Sloman to tell me that our contract had been terminated.

I was out of a job. But frankly, I was relieved, as was my wife. We did not enjoy living in Athens, and I was beginning to feel unwelcome and finding the job quite tedious. Jim had managed to secure a six month termination salary for his team, which was very satisfactory. So, we returned to Brisbane.

Why the Olympics.

My time with the Olympics was interesting. I believe that I took on the role because I was unsettled after the New Delhi debacle, and because of the high profile aspect of the Olympics. I had spent many fulfilling years in the Hyatt organisation, and met and worked with a number of great people. But I had difficulty gaining further traction with my career. Yes, I had chosen to stay in Coolum while my children were developing, but I had also indicated on a number of occasions that I would be prepared to take on any position which would further my career. Unfortunately, I seemed to be typecast as the 'resort guy' and, apart from the aborted prospect in Delhi, I was not offered any other roles. This I found strange, given that I had performed satisfactorily in all my roles to date, with Coolum being a particularly difficult challenge. In addition, I had been nominated as the company's General Manager of the year on two occasions, which was, of course, an honour, but again did not lead to further consideration. Perhaps I had not been pushy enough and thought that my betters would eventually come to recognise my contribution. I have no doubt that many people in the corporate world feel the same way! In any case, this was my mindset when I was approached initially about the Olympics role in Sydney. I was keen to take on a new challenge but opportunities with Hyatt seemed limited at that time.

Consulting.

Upon returning from Athens, I spent some time in Brisbane working as a consultant for various clients. These included private hotel owners, developers and golf club organisations. This work tended to be spasmodic, and not entirely satisfying. In addition, lots of clients search for information, but are reluctant to pay for it. There was one exception.

Vaughan Bullivant was the reluctant owner of a hotel resort on Day Dream Island, one of the Australian Whitsunday islands. I say reluctant, as Vaughan somehow ended up owning the resort by default. In his early life, Vaughan had been a water ski champion, who was severely injured, and almost died, in a water ski accident. When in hospital he followed his regimen of consuming lots of vitamins, which he claims saved his life, and restored his health. As a result, he purchased a small vitamin business, which he expanded into a national brand and later sold for $135 million. He was home free, or so he thought.

Vaughan had once worked for a mercurial figure by the name of Keith Williams. Keith was a larger than life character, who owned and operated many businesses in his native Queensland. He could be quite intimidating and had a certain hold over Vaughan, who somehow had never managed to get out from under Keith's authority. So, as Vaughan was enjoying his new-found wealth, he received a call from Keith with the news that Day Dream Island was for sale for the throwaway price of $12 million. The previous owners had spent almost $100 million on redeveloping the island, but could not make a go of it. Keith felt that it was a steal, and that he and Vaughan should enter into a 50-50 deal to purchase it.

Vaughan initially rejected the idea, saying that he was now comfortably off, and did not want the headache of owning a resort island. He also pleaded ignorance of the resort and hospitality business. However, Keith could be very persuasive and he just about bullied Vaughan into agreeing to proceed with the purchase. The deal was arranged, but when it came to settling Keith asked Vaughan to pay the whole $12 million and that he, Keith, would reimburse him. Vaughan foolishly went ahead and settled but when he later asked Keith for his share, Keith took umbrage, suggesting that Vaughan did not trust him. He became angry and told Vaughan that they were no longer partners and that he, Vaughan, was now the sole owner of the island.

This was quite devastating to Vaughan and caused him all sorts of stress. The island resort was losing $600,000 per month with no resolution in sight. The operation was poorly managed with unqualified managers and staff. Vaughan had no idea where to begin. This was where I came in through the request of Vaughan's lawyer and advisor. I went so have a chat with Vaughan in his palatial mansion by the sea in Brisbane. He was very anxious and totally stressed by the mess he'd gotten into. He told me that it was literally driving him to drink, and that he was continually hung over as a result. He had also developed a nervous cough! I must say that I liked Vaughan and could sympathise with his situation. Despite his dilemma, he was kind in his dealings. He asked me to visit the island and to make some recommendations. This I did, and I believe that I helped Vaughan crystallise his thoughts on the way forward. I believe that he eventually made a success of the venture and that his island became a very popular tourist destination.

Borneo

One rather memorable consulting role took me to the fabled island of Borneo. My very good friend, Richard White, was the Vice President of Preferred Hotels. This organisation represents and markets luxury hotels which are not aligned with a corporate organisation. The owner of a resort hotel on an island just off the coast, close to the city of Kota Kinabalu, had requested representation from Preferred Hotels. Kota Kinabalu is in the Malaysian province of Sabah.

Richard was worried about the standard of the resort he had been asked to represent. He had visited and felt the resort required a significant upgrade in facilities, service, and management, before his company would consider representation. The owner was prepared to follow Richard's recommendations. Richard felt that he needed some advice from an experienced resort operator, and asked me to travel to Kinabalu to review the resort operation. He kindly suggested that I could include my wife, Cathie, on the trip.

We travelled from Brisbane via Singapore and onwards to Kota Kinabalu, where we were met by resort staff and escorted on a launch to the island. I have to say that we found Kota Kinabalu to be a very attractive place, set on the shores of the South China Sea, with beautiful beaches, and surrounded by rain forest.

The resort was located on a beautiful island paradise. Most of the island was national park, with the resort nestled by a pristine beach, where the balmy lukewarm water was relatively shallow, and a delight for swimming. We were checked in to a villa set in the rainforest. In fact, the villas were generally quite enveloped by the forest. So much so that the monkeys, and all sorts of other animals, made frequent visits to our balcony.

However, there were indeed many deficiencies with the resort operation. I set about my review and made copious recommendations on what was necessary in order to upgrade the facility to international standard. The owner had developed the resort for his daughter, who had studied hospitality in Melbourne. Unfortunately, there had not been much expertise in either design, construction, or management, so it was an uphill battle.

The owner was one of Sabah's wealthiest individuals. He was quite the environmentalist and had developed a cutting edge marine research institute on a nearby island. At this facility his scientists had developed a method of regenerating coral and transplanting it in the sea. This was critical to the survival of the giant clam which was being fished to extinction, and was also losing its habitat with the deterioration of the coral. This was most impressive and he is to be congratulated for this wonderful work.

We were invited to visit the research facility and duly embarked on a speed boat from our island paradise. We were very impressed with the work in regenerating the coral and thereby the life of the clams. There was, however, quite an interruption to our tour of the facility. At the time of our visit there had been an uprising by the followers of the Sultan of Sulu against the Malaysian authorities.

By way of background, Sulu was once upon a time a sultanate which encompassed parts of Borneo, Indonesia and The Philippines. The title of Sultan had been handed down over the ages with little or no authority. However, for some time the most recent Sultan and his followers had been railing against the Malaysian government over various injustices, which they felt they had suffered. This led to a serious incident where two Malaysian police personnel had been shot and killed. The government reacted quite aggressively and in a confrontation twelve of the Sulu followers were shot dead. This further enraged an already volatile situation.

We received word that the Sultans followers were approaching the island and we were advised to retire to Kota Kinabalu post haste, as our host was worried that we could be taken hostage. We did just that and, in James Bond fashion, we sped across the sea in our maxed out speed boat. We took up residence in a penthouse owned by the resort owner and were told not to go outside unless we were accompanied by security. Food and drink was provided in the penthouse, but one evening we decided to go to the Westin hotel to have dinner. The Westin was owned by our client, the resort owner.

We were chauffeured by a driver who had all the appearances of a special forces operative. Heavily built, crew cut, and very obviously packing a fire arm. We almost had a pleasant dinner at the Westin except we were again interrupted and advised to return to our accommodation, as the Sulu people were rumoured to have infiltrated the town. So we had another quick getaway courtesy of our special forces escort.

Next day all seemed to be calm and we departed for home. I completed my report but am not aware that any of my recommendations were enacted. When I was growing up in Ireland we used to talk about the scary wild man from Borneo, not having a clue as to where Borneo might be. Little did I think that one day I would be there, and threatened by the wild man!

Back to Coolum

In 2003 the Lend Lease Corporation purchased the Hyatt Regency Coolum from Kumagai Gumi. As a major residential developer, Lend Lease identified the 150 hectare land bank which existed at the resort, and sought to embark on a significant housing development.

In essence, this was in keeping with the original development plans, which were never realised by Kumagai Gumi. Fundamentally, the resort operation required very significant revenue streams in order to be viable and the housing development was intended to be a major contributor.

Unfortunately, Kumagai did not have the stomach for further development, given the nightmares they experienced with the complicated ownership structure. Lend Lease on the other hand had recently completed a housing development at the neighbouring Twin Waters resort which had been very successful. In fact, the market was so strong that they could not build the houses quickly enough. They sought similar success at the Hyatt.

I received an invitation to meet with Murray Middleton, then the Lend Lease project manager for the Sunshine Coast, including the Coolum development. Murray indicated that he was somewhat concerned with the Coolum management and asked me if I would be prepared to review the operation. I must say that I felt a little bit uncomfortable at the prospect of returning to the resort as an owner's representative. I wondered what the reaction of Hyatt would be. But I was interested in the role and felt that I could certainly contribute, given my long history with the property. I duly arranged to visit the resort and had some discussions in a joint meeting with the Lend Lease and Hyatt representatives.

There was very poor chemistry between the two teams. The Hyatt manager seemed to take umbrage with the Lend Lease involvement and obviously felt that the Lend Lease representatives were over stepping the mark by their involvement in the operation. As I have said previously, this is very often a source of contention between management companies and owners, and requires careful management lest it create irreversible enmity and infighting.

A manager, while equipped with the security of a management contract, must be flexible and understanding of the owning companies aspirations. A spirit of cooperation is absolutely critical to the overall success of the enterprise. This was obviously not the case at Coolum.

It didn't take long before I was again approached by Murray Middleton, who indicated that Lend Lease were about to inform Hyatt that they wanted a change of general manager. Murray asked me if I would be prepared to return to the role. This was somewhat of a surprise and I said that I needed a little time to consider. What had struck me on my recent visit to the resort was the fact that it was beginning to show its age. It was now 15 years old and required renewal. A significant programme of refurbishment was necessary in all areas.

I mentioned this to Murray, and made it a condition of my return to the property. I was assured that it was the intention of Lend Lease to embark on a major renewal programme, as the success of their residential development would depend, to a great extent, on the quality of the resort facilities. This sounded a logical and very sound policy.

So I agreed to return to my old stomping grounds! But first I needed to clear the way with Hyatt so I contacted their regional office and explained the situation. The response was encouraging and I believe that Hyatt was quite happy to have me back in the role again, as they were already experiencing some difficulties with the new owning company.

In early 2004 I returned to my old job, old office, old house, and an ageing resort. I was quite enthused and delighted to be back 'home'. I had put my life and soul into the property over the previous 10 year period, and I felt that I could reenergise the organisation. In this regard, the bottom line had been deteriorating as competition grew, and customers had started to comment on the ageing facilities. This was a major concern. In addition, the service levels had dropped somewhat requiring a complete refocus. I embarked on this with gusto and I am pleased to say that the staff and management responded positively. Customer comments improved and many former customers were returning. I was encouraged.

However, Lend Lease development activity was starting to have an impact on what was a very pristine environment. Unfortunately, they had become fixated on rearranging the golf course so that they could build houses on the beachside, where they would generate better prices. This involved relocating the five golf holes on the beach side to the western side of the resort, which was essentially a rain forest. Apart from the desecration of the rain forest, this project involved massive and very expensive earthworks, which obviously had an impact on the general peace and quiet. This work lasted some 18 months. In my opinion, and that of the course designer, Robert Trent Jones, this was an unfortunate development, which somewhat compromised the golf course layout. It was also rather ill judged, as the rain forest area was essentially a swamp requiring enormous earthworks to make it amenable to constructing golf holes. It cost Lend Lease a considerable amount of money to relocate the five holes simply so they could exact more money from the beachside, which did not eventuate in the end. I found this overall strategy quite perplexing, considering that approval was already in place to construct houses along the fairways of the holes on the beach side. However, the prospect of removing the holes to make way for more houses, and better prices, was too tempting to resist. This was an unfortunate and rather opportunistic decision which greatly detracted from the overall ambience of the resort.

I felt compelled to keep reminding Lend Lease of the need to commence work on a refurbishing programme. I was encouraged when plans were drawn up to redesign and refurbish the resort spa which was an essential element of the overall offering. This project was successfully completed resulting in a much improved facility.

However, there seemed to be no further appetite for addressing other areas such as bedrooms and restaurants. This concerned me, as the condition of the rooms in particular was having a negative effect on business levels. I constantly relayed this fact to the Lend Lease representatives but met with a certain intransigence, suggesting that there was no real intention to embark on a major refurbishment. It seemed that their strategy was to focus on the aspects which affected their housing development and sales, and to defer any investment in the resort facilities, with the exception of the spa.

This made some commercial sense in their considerations, as their housing clients would tend to be impressed with a state of the art spa, with little regard or use for the resort bedrooms. I began to feel that I had been sold a pup! The strategy became obvious to me, and I could do nothing about it. Murray Middleton had moved on, and I was now dealing with a different team, who simply had no interest in discussing any substantial refurbishment plan. They did embark on having what is referred to as a mock up room designed and completed, but only ever got around to actually refurbishing nine rooms.

In an effort to persuade Lend Lease to reconsider their position, I developed and presented a business plan to them which showed a very reasonable return on investment were they to refurbish the resort, construct a conference facility, and complete the housing development. The numbers in the plan were very conservative and, I felt, easily achievable. In fact, I invited Lend Lease to challenge me on any and all assumptions but I did not receive a response. This confirmed my suspicion that their tenure was meant to be short term. The resort was now losing money with the customer base steadily decreasing. In addition, the housing market had entered a downturn and Lend Lease were now in a difficult situation faced with accumulating losses at the resort, and a dwindling housing market. I found this to be a particularly depressing period.

New Owner

Clive Palmer is a larger than life Australian business identity. Clive owned a house at The Lakes precinct which neighboured the resort. He was a regular customer. He and his extended family regularly spent Christmas enjoying the resorts festive activities. One Sunday morning I received a call from Clive advising me that he had bought the resort. I was quite flabbergasted, as I'd had no advice whatsoever from Lend Lease. I congratulated Clive and said that I looked forward to working with him. Little did I know what was in store.

For a period of one year my interaction with Clive was respectful and I have to say that he did not unduly interfere in the operation. He did appoint a number of apparatchiks from his mining business to liaise with myself and other members of the management team. These individuals had little or no knowledge of the hospitality industry and were simply focused on reacting to directions from Clive. We held many meetings which were to absolutely no avail with endless discussions on things like the cost of food, the price of rooms, restaurant opening hours, and even the frequency of mowing of the golf course. Generally pointless activity which seemed to make these owners representatives feel they were making a contribution.

The resort continued to lose money with customers drifting away to other destinations. I presented my business plan with ample examples of customer feedback, citing the need for a major refurbishment programme. This, unfortunately, fell on deaf ears, and the losses continued to mount.

Tahiti

One day Clive advised me that he was keen to explore investment opportunities in Tahiti. He had arranged to meet the President of Tahiti and was intending to inspect some resorts, which were on the market. I found this to be quite strange considering that he was not prepared to invest in renewing Coolum, which was a much more viable option than some pipe dream in Tahiti. In any case, Clive requested that I join him on the trip, and that I request the presence of the Hyatt Vice President for Australia, Robert Dawson.

Robert was somewhat taken aback when I relayed the invitation, and he was as perplexed as I was on the prospect of purchasing resorts in Tahiti. It is a beautiful destination, but access is expensive, difficult, and time consuming. It is a destination for the well heeled but not a thriving one. It also suffers economically and is subsidised by the French government.

This turned out to be some trip, I must say. We boarded Clive's private jet at Brisbane airport and flew to New Caledonia, where Clive had a mining operation. There were 10 people on board including Clive's lovely wife, Anna, who busied herself serving snacks to the passengers. We then headed to the Cook Islands where we refuelled, and thence to Papeete, the capital of Tahiti, where we stayed at the Hilton.

Clive and his wife had been invited to lunch with the President, a charming individual who was a native Tahitian, and somewhat of a revolutionary. This gentleman had a fervent dislike for his French masters, and had been voted in and out as President on a number of occasions.

Clive asked one of his local handlers to contact the President's office, and advise that he would like to bring along eight extra guests to the lunch. This of course was somewhat unusual, but in the true spirit of Tahitian hospitality we were all invited to come along. We had a very pleasant lunch after which the President said some words to the effect that he was delighted that a businessman of Mr Palmer's stature was considering investing in his country.

The President then mentioned that there happened to be an island in Tahiti which was made up almost entirely of phosphate, and that he would appreciate Mr Palmer's mining expertise in realising that resource. I think I then understood Clive's interest in Tahiti! Clive was then asked to reply to the President's gracious words, which he did admirably. In fact, knowing his audience, Clive stated that Australians and Tahitians were 'brothers in the Pacific' and did not need colonial despots interfering in the affairs of the region. The President was delighted with these words!

We then travelled to the fabled and stunningly beautiful island of Bora Bora. Clive had arranged accommodation in the various luxury resorts, with he and his wife staying at the Four Seasons, and others in the party at different locations. I think we were meant to compare notes! Robert Dawson and I were lodged in magnificent over water chalets at the St Regis. The chalets featured glass floors for observing the reef and the tropical fish, as well as balconies from which we simply dived into the lagoon as our morning wake up. It was fabulous. However, we were somewhat uneasy when we went to dinner, as we then realised that every table in the restaurant was occupied by honeymoon couples. And here we were, two males looking all the world like a couple. We received some interesting looks from both the head waiter, and the happy couples.

Resorts for Sale

One of our retinue was a real estate agent from Australia, who Clive had asked to identify resorts which were for sale. This individual did a lot of groundwork investigating the ownership of the various resorts, and indicating that he had an interested buyer should any of them wish to sell. Of course, most things are for sale if the price is right. In any case, we spent a day touring various resort properties, including what was once the Bora Bora Hilton. This facility was no longer in operation, and Hilton were keen to be relieved of it.

They understood that Clive was very interested and saw this as the opportunity they had been waiting on for many years. To demonstrate their enthusiasm, Hilton had arranged for two of their Vice Presidents to be present for the inspection, and to meet Mr Palmer. One vice president travelled from Sydney, and the other from Hong Kong. No mean feat considering how difficult and time consuming it is to get to Bora Bora.

It was arranged that we would meet at the now defunct Hilton for the inspection. We travelled to the site by motor launch, where the Hilton representatives and the rest of our group were waiting at the jetty to welcome Clive. It was quite hot and the two Hilton executives were in suits. We waited quite a long time before Clive's launch eventually arrived. Clive stepped out onto the Jetty which was about 50 metres long. He looked around, glanced at the ramshackle and defunct resort, waved at our welcoming party, and returned to his launch. He then took off over the horizon leaving the two Hilton executives very unimpressed, and quite hot under the collar. They had made a very long and time consuming trip for nothing, not even the pleasure of meeting the great man!

A Row with Hyatt.

While my dealings with Clive Palmer had always been courteous, I suppose I should have anticipated that a man like Clive couldn't abide having one of his assets managed by a third party, over whom he had little control. Like any management company's operating method, the management contract under which Hyatt managed the Hyatt Regency Coolum, was strictly drafted to protect the rights of Hyatt, and to provide discretion in managing the unit. The owner was certainly respected, but the relationship was never intended to form a partnership. Hyatt jealously protected its independence for good reason. This independence, however, can create friction with certain owners who are determined to impose their will the operation. Oft times, the owners opinion on matters relating to customer service can be less than appropriate. Whereas, Hyatt would consider that they are the experts in such matters and should be left to manage without undue interference. This situation can be a recipe for confrontation, regardless of the flexibility of the local unit manager, who is charged with fostering good relations with owner.

Clive sent an explosive letter to Hyatt headquarters, accusing them of stealing sixty million dollars from the resort over the life of the management contract, approximately 25 years. Obviously, this accusation caused mayhem in the world of Hyatt, a respected international company listed on the New York stock exchange. I received a call from a Hyatt lawyer in Chicago who said to me 'who the fuck is Clive Palmer and who does he think he is. I will take this guy to the cleaners for this false and vicious accusation'.

Clive initiated proceedings to terminate the management contract and Hyatt, of course, responded. And so we were listed to fight the case in the Supreme Court of Queensland. I was required to make a statement and spent a day in the office of Hyatt's Brisbane lawyers. My statement was transmitted to Clive's lawyers and onward to Clive. Within hours, I received a voice mail message from Clive stating the following ' Maurice, you are fired. You have two weeks to get out of the company house, which you are occupying, and you are persona non gratis at the resort, with immediate effect. You will not receive any food and beverage or housekeeping services'. What a shock!

However, there is a humorous side to most things, and in this case a reporter from the Sunshine Coast newspaper was informed of my treatment. The next day the front page headline read 'Clive Refuses to Feed GM'. Despite, however, the directive from Clive to curtail any services to the Holland household, we were quite humbled by the efforts of the resort management team who continued to deliver the necessities.

The following day I informed the Hyatt barrister of my dismissal and treatment. The Barrister took the view that Clive had intimidated a witness of the court and said that he would 'send him to jail' for this offence. However, just prior to the opening of court proceedings, Clive asked the judge for permission to speak. He stated that Mr Holland had not been dismissed as a result of his witness statement, but for operational reasons.

This did not impress the judge, who stated ' Mr Palmer, you have no right to dismiss Mr Holland, as he was appointed by Hyatt, and as far as this court is concerned, Mr Holland is reinstated with immediate effect'. Round one to Hyatt.

Throughout this interesting saga I had been impressing on Hyatt the need to compromise, and to reach a settlement. It was very obvious that Palmer could not abide Hyatt or any other management company controlling his resort. Best to acknowledge this and move on. Hyatt eventually came around to this realisation and negotiated a termination arrangement with Clive, to end Hyatt's involvement and no further litigation.

So, we were given one month to end Hyatt's 25 years of association with the resort. I duly tidied things up, packed my belongings and departed. A very sad ending, I must say. I had contributed my whole being into the struggle to make the place viable and was sad that I had not succeeded.

Unfortunately, the Hyatt Coolum never really had an enlightened owner who could realise the true potential. We had spent years building the brand and commanded great loyalty in the market place. What was required was expansive thinking but this, alas, was sadly missing. Too many uninformed consultants had imposed their shallow thinking on the project over too many years. In the end, what could have become a thriving resort destination was left to wither. After a few years of self managing, Clive Palmer eventually closed the resort. It was a magnificent failure.

Brisbane and Indooroopilly

Hyatt asked me to take on the task of simultaneously opening two resorts in China, but I was not inclined to relocate, or to spend time in China. I took up residence in Brisbane after my departure from Coolum. Brisbane is a really pleasant city which has matured into quite the cosmopolitan society, with ample social outlets, quality theatre, abundance of good and modern restaurants, and very manageable traffic. In short, it's a nice place to live.

I have been, and still am, a member of Indooroopilly Golf Club. This is a rather grand facility with 36 holes of golf, and located on the banks of the Brisbane river. It is by far the premier golfing facility in the city, with 2000 members. The club was experiencing some management upheaval with the board and management in conflict. The upshot was the rather sudden departure of the club Chief Executive Officer. I was vaguely aware of this rather disruptive situation, but was not involved.

However, I was approached by members of the board asking me to "hold the fort' as CEO, until such time as a permanent replacement could be identified. I was somewhat reluctant to embark on such a mission, as I was enjoying my golf and life in Brisbane, which I did not want to compromise. Discussions, however, suggested that the role would be short term, and that I would be assisting the club out of its difficult situation. This somewhat appealed to my sense of duty! So, I accepted the challenge and took on the role of Acting CEO of Indooroopilly Golf Club.

This turned out to be quite a challenge. As a member with a background in hospitality and resorts, I was conscious of many service and presentation deficiencies at the club. The need for hands on management was apparent. However, I was not entirely aware of the fact that the club was struggling financially. Some significant debt had been incurred and membership and business levels were deteriorating. The club was operating at a financial loss. Such a situation always creates stress and can be difficult to correct. Board members with the best will in the world offered all sorts of remedies, and tended to be disappointed if their suggestions were not acted upon.

Cutting costs is always a knee jerk reaction, to be avoided unless there are very obvious cost overruns. The danger with indiscriminate cost cutting is that it can lower the quality of the product, and further alienate the clientele. The obvious answer was to increase revenue. To do this there was the basic need of tidying, painting and cleaning a facility which had been allowed to deteriorate. Gardens were also in need of attention. In addition, service levels had to be improved in order to arrest what was becoming a poor and damaging reputation. Clients had had poor experiences with food and service, adding to a generally negative perception of the club. Obviously, this perception was affecting membership numbers.

I had never previously managed a members organisation. This took some adjustment on my part, as I was used to making management decisions without much referral. In a club situation, there is a President, Captain, and board members who all feel they have a right to know. And I suppose they have! However, my style is quite direct and once I have decided on a direction or philosophy, I can be difficult to dissuade. This trait led to some friction, I must admit. However, when one is immersed in a difficult struggle, and one feels that one knows how to retrieve the situation, then one is reluctant to be distracted!

In any case, after some months in the role, I was somewhat vindicated when customer comments started to improve, revenues increased, and membership enquiries took an upward trend. Months merged into years and without really being conscious of the time which had elapsed, I had spent over two years in a job I had taken on for three months. I was conscious that things had improved at the club and I was deriving some satisfaction from this achievement. I had also become friendly with many of the members, which was a pleasant bonus. After a period of two years and seven months I decided that it was time to resign my temporary position and return to being a member.

Now

So, where to from here....

It is now June 2019. Last year my beloved brother, Sean, died from motor neurone desease. This was a terrible shock and it was awful to see such a fine and elegant man deteriorate so fast. It also put things in perspective and reminded me of our mortality. How often are we reminded to count our blessings? How often do we abide by that advice? It is all too easy to be distracted by irritants and inconsequential matters. It is important to focus on simple things, and to enjoy what is left, for we know not how much is left.

I am trying to take time to read, walk, talk, play, wander and wonder. Trying to stop worrying, and to smile more. It's not easy, though. It takes a conscious effort. But it is very worthwhile.

Just a Simple Innkeeper.

Brisbane 2019

www.ingramcontent.com/pod-product-compliance
Lightning Source LLC
Chambersburg PA
CBHW071611080526
44588CB00010B/1092